SIDE BY SIDE
ACTIVITY WORKBOOK

1A

Steven J. Molinsky

Bill Bliss

Illustrated by

Richard E. Hill

Contributing Authors

Elizabeth Handley
with
Mary Ann Perry
Christine Harvey

Editorial Development

Tina B. Carver

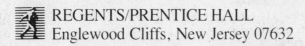
REGENTS/PRENTICE HALL
Englewood Cliffs, New Jersey 07632

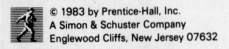
Printed in the United States of America

20 19 18 17

ISBN 0-13-809525-6

Prentice-Hall International (UK) Limited, *London*
Prentice-Hall of Australia Pty. Limited, *Sydney*
Prentice-Hall Canada Inc., *Toronto*
Prentice-Hall Hispanoamericana, S.A., *Mexico*
Prentice-Hall of India Private Limited, *New Delhi*
Prentice-Hall of Japan, Inc., *Tokyo*
Simon & Schuster Asia Pte. Ltd., *Singapore*
Editora Prentice-Hall do Brasil, Ltda., *Rio de Janeiro*

Contents

A. WHAT ARE THEY SAYING?

what	my	name	from	I
is	your	address	thank	you
am		phone number		

1. What is your name? — My *name is* Betty Jones.

2. What is your address? — My address is 333 Main Street.

3. What is your phone number? — My phone number is 868-2766.

4. thank you. — You're welcome.

5. What is your name?

My name is Kiamadis.

6. what is your address?

My address is _____

Harry Ross
10 River Street

1

7. _____ My _____ name _____ is _____ Kianadis Jurado _____ ?

My phone number _is_ 723-1576.

8. Where are _____ from? _____ Chicago.

B. NAME/ADDRESS/PHONE NUMBER

What is YOUR name, address, and phone number?

STUDENT IDENTIFICATION CARD
Name: _Maria_   _Gonzalez_
First Name   Last Name
Address: _235 Main Street_
Number   Street
Phone _741-8906_
Number:

STUDENT IDENTIFICATION CARD
Name: _Kianadis Jurado_
First Name   Last Name
Address: _6 Brookside Pba_
Number   Street
Phone _My telyon is_
Number: _546-7876_

My name is Maria Gonzalez.
My address is 235 Main Street.
My phone number is 741-8906.

_My_ _name_ _is_ Kianadis Jurado
My address is 6 Brookside Place
My phone number is 546-7876

| one | two | three | four | five | six | seven | eight | nine | ten |

C. WRITE

1 = _one_   4 = _four_   7 = _seven_

2 = _two_   5 = _five_   8 = _eight_

3 = _three_   6 = _six_   9 = _nine_

              ✳   10 = _ten_

D. WHAT'S THE NUMBER?

3. My address is seven Main Street. _7_

4. My address is five Main Street. _5_

1. My address is four Main Street.

5. My address is nine Main Street. _9_

2. My address is ten Main Street. _10_

6. My address is eight Main Street. _8_

E. LISTEN   Listen and write the missing number.

1.
What is your phone number?

My phone number is 231-496 _5_.

2.
What is your phone number?

My phone number is 743-529 _____.

3.
What is your phone number?

My phone number is 492-71 _____ 5.

4.
What is your phone number?

My phone number is 637-89 _____ 6.

F. LISTEN

Listen and put a circle around the number you hear.

1. | 1 | ③ | 5 |

2. | 6 | 7 | 8 |

3. | 4 | 5 | 6 |

4. | 5 | 7 | 10 |

5. | 6 | 8 | 9 |

6. | 2 | 3 | 6 |

A. WHAT ARE THEY SAYING?

I'm	you	basement	living room
we're	are	bedroom	yard
they're	where	kitchen	

2

1.
Where are you?

I'm in the garage.

2.
Where _are_ you?

We're in the _living_ _room_.

3.
Where _are_ Harry and Betty?

They're in the _yard_.

4.
Where _are_ you and Tom?

Where in the _bedroom_.

5.
Where _are_ John and Bill?

_He_ in the _basement_.

6.
Where _are_ you?

_He is_ in the _dining room_.

B. WHAT ARE THEY SAYING?

where's	she's	living room	kitchen
he's	it's	garage	

1. *Where's* Fred?
   He's in the _kitchen_ .

2. _She is_ Helen?
   She is in the _living room_ .

3. _He is in the_ the car?
   _He is_ in the _garage_ .

C. WHERE ARE THEY?

we	he	they
	she	
	it	

(Mr. and Mrs. Jones) 1. _They_ are in the dining room.

(Helen) 2. _she_ is in the living room.

(Mr. Nelson) 3. _he_ is in the bedroom.

(Fred and Tom) 4. _We_ are in the bedroom.

(Betty and I) 5. _They_ are in the garage.

(The newspaper) 6. _it_ is in the bedroom.

(John) 7. _he_ is in the bathroom.

(Mrs. Wilson) 8. _he_ is in the basement.

(The cat) 9. _it_ is in the yard.

D. WHERE ARE THEY?

I'm	we're	he's	where's
	you're	she's	
	they're	it's	

(He is) 1. _He's_ in the garage.

(I am) 2. _I'am_ in the kitchen.

(We are) 3. _We'are_ in the bedroom.

(You are) 4. _aYou'are_ in the dining room.

(She is) 5. _she'is_ in the living room.

(Where is) 6. _Where'is_ the newspaper?

(It is) 7. _It'is_ in the basement.

(They are) 8. _They'are_ in the yard.

5

THE FRANKLIN FAMILY

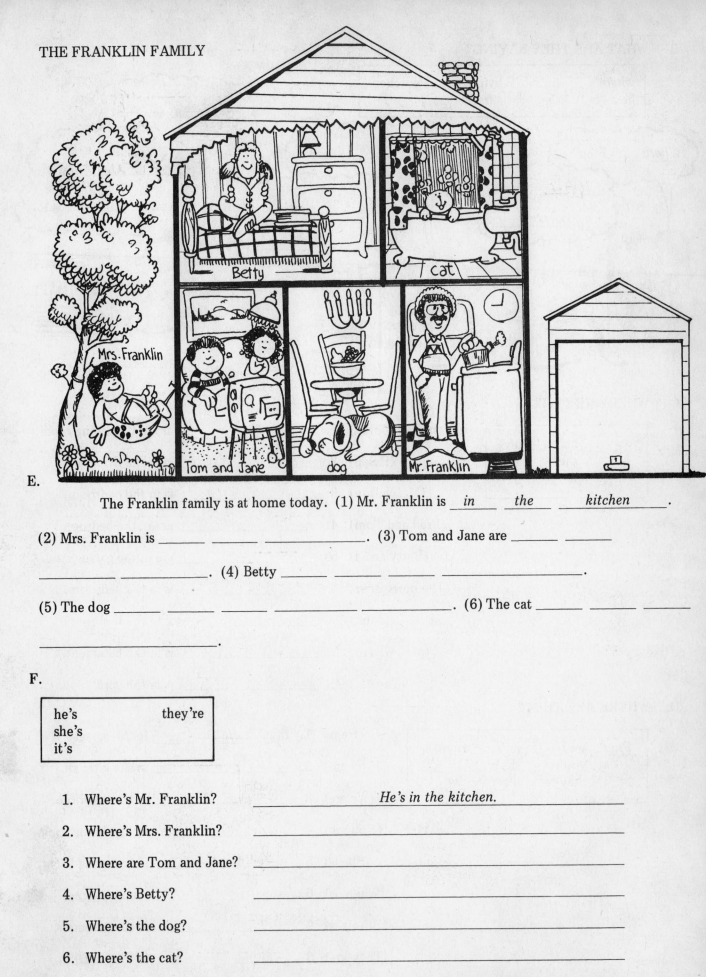

E.

The Franklin family is at home today. (1) Mr. Franklin is ___in___ ___the___ ___kitchen___ .

(2) Mrs. Franklin is _____ _____ _____ . (3) Tom and Jane are _____ _____

_____ _____ . (4) Betty _____ _____ _____ _____ .

(5) The dog _____ _____ _____ _____ _____ . (6) The cat _____ _____ _____

_____ .

F.

he's	they're
she's	
it's	

1. Where's Mr. Franklin? _____*He's in the kitchen.*_____

2. Where's Mrs. Franklin? _____

3. Where are Tom and Jane? _____

4. Where's Betty? _____

5. Where's the dog? _____

6. Where's the cat? _____

6

G. WHAT'S THE SIGN?

Fill in the signs. Then complete the sentences.

1. Tom and Mary _____*are in the library*_____ .

2. Albert is _____ _____ .

3. Fred and Helen are _____ _____ .

4. Betty _____ _____ .

5. Rita _____ _____ .

6. Bob and Jane _____ _____ .

7. Jane _____ _____ .

8. John and Martha _____ _____ .

7

H. LISTEN

Listen to each sentence. Put a check (√) next to the appropriate picture.

I. LISTEN

Listen to the following conversations. Put a circle around the right word.

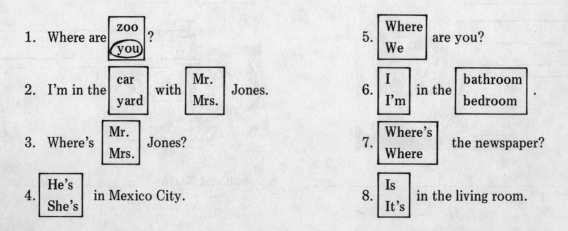

1. Where are [zoo / (you)]?

2. I'm in the [car / yard] with [Mr. / Mrs.] Jones.

3. Where's [Mr. / Mrs.] Jones?

4. [He's / She's] in Mexico City.

5. [Where / We] are you?

6. [I / I'm] in the [bathroom / bedroom].

7. [Where's / Where] the newspaper?

8. [Is / It's] in the living room.

8

A. WHAT ARE THEY SAYING?

doing	I'm	you
cooking	he's	the dog
sleeping	she's	what
studying	it's	what's
watching	they're	are

3

1.
What are you doing?
I'm reading.

2.
What _____ _____ doing?
We're _____.

3.
What _____ Mary and Fred _____?
_____ _____ English.

4.
What's Tom _____?
_____ eating.

5.
_____ Martha _____?
_____ _____ TV.

6.
What's _____ _____?
_____ _____.

9

B. WHAT ARE THEY DOING?

dancing	listening	singing
drinking	playing	sleeping
eating	reading	watching

1. He's _____reading._____

2. She's _____ .

3. They're _____ .

4. He's _____ .

5. She's _____ to the radio.

6. They're _____ cards.

7. He's _____ .

8. They're _____ coffee.

9. She's _____ TV.

C. LISTEN

Listen to each sentence. Put a check (√) next to the appropriate picture.

1.

2.

3.

4.

5.

6.

7.

8.

D. WHAT'S THE QUESTION?

Where is { he / she / it } ?   What's { he / she / it } doing?

Where are { you / they } ?   What are { you / they } doing?

1. _Where___ _are___ _you___ ?   I'm in the bedroom.

2. _What's___ _she___ _doing___ ?   She's playing cards.

3. _____ ?   He's in the discotheque.

4. _____ ?   I'm studying English.

5. _____ ?   He's eating breakfast.

6. _____ ?   They're in the bank.

7. _____ ?   We're in the library.

8. _____ ?   It's in the garage.

9. _____ ?   She's in the park.

10. _____ ?   It's sleeping.

11. _____ ?   They're playing baseball.

12. 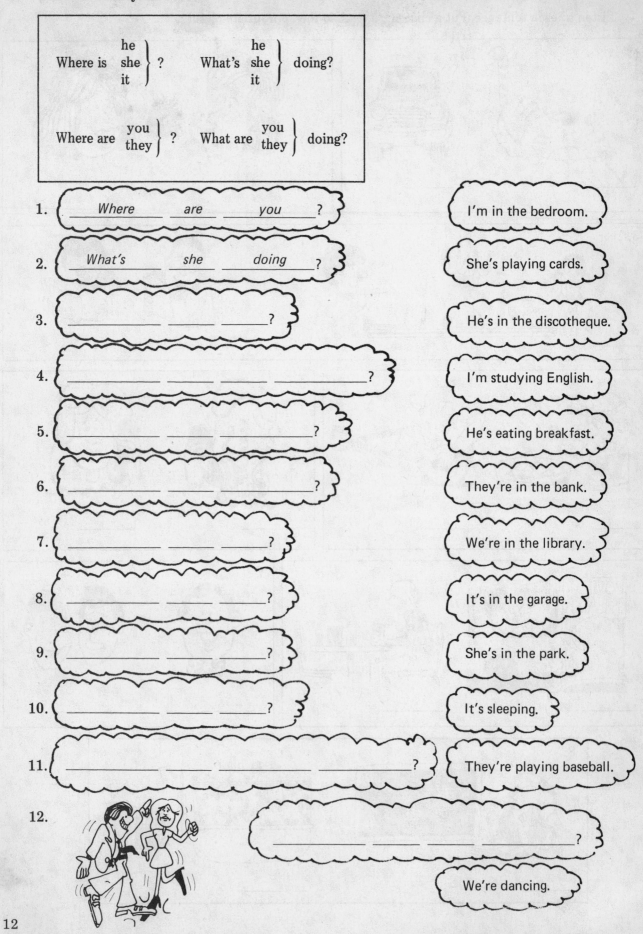 _____ ?

We're dancing.

12

CHECK-UP TEST: Chapters 1-3

A.   Answer the questions.

Ex.   What's your telephone number?

My ___telephone number is 236-2558___ .

1.   What's your name?

My _____ .

2.   What's your address?

My _____ .

3.   Where are you from?

I _____ .

B.   Put a circle around the correct answer.

Ex.   The car is in the [(garage) / hospital / supermarket] .

1.   Walter is eating [restaurant / coffee / breakfast] .

2.   Where's Tom? [He's / You're / She's] in the bedroom.

3.   The monkey is in the [bank / post office / zoo] .

4.   Where are you? [They're / We're / He's] in the living room.

5.   Albert is in the library. He's [cooking / dancing / reading] .

6.   Miss Jackson is drinking [dining room / cafeteria / coffee] .

7.   Jane is playing [cards / car / yard] .

C.   Fill in the blanks.

Ex.   They're __in__ the bedroom.

1.   _____ are you? I'm in the yard.

2.   What's Helen _____? She's sleeping.

3.   Tom is _____ the garage.

4.   What's Miss Jones doing? _____ singing.

5.   Where's the newspaper? _____ in the kitchen.

6.   Walter _____ Mary are in the bank.

7.   She's _____ TV.

8.   Bobby is _____ to the radio.

9.   _____ are Mr. and Mrs. Smith doing?

10.   Where are you and Tom? _____ in the park.

D.   Listen and write the number you hear.

Ex.   547-2 _6_ 31

1.   695-33 _____ 2

2.   49 _____ -8577

3.   7 _____ 4-0681

4.   358-967 _____

5.   582-41 _____ 6

A. ON THE PHONE

what	her	my	cleaning	children
what's	his	our	doing	homework
are		their	fixing	sink

1.

Hi! _____What_____ are you doing?

I'm fixing __my__ __sink__ .

2.

What's Bob _____?

He's _____ _____ car.

3.

_____ Mary doing?

She's cleaning _____ room.

4.

_____ _____ you doing?

We're _____

_____ apartment.

5.

What are your _____ doing?

They're doing _____ _____ .

14

B. WHAT'S THE WORD?

my	our
his	your
her	their
its	

1. I'm fixing _____my_____ sink.

2. We're cleaning _____ yard.

3. Nancy is washing _____ car.

4. Mr. and Mrs. Jones are doing _____ exercises.

5. Henry is feeding _____ cat.

6. The dog is eating _____ dinner.

7. You're doing _____ homework.

C. PUZZLE

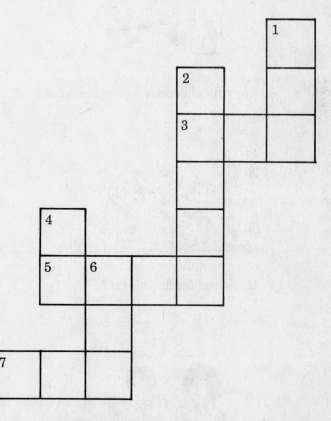

Across

3. Albert is brushing _his_ teeth.

5. You're fixing _____ bicycle.

7. Maria is cleaning _____ room.

Down

1. The cat is eating _____ breakfast.

2. Mr. and Mrs. Thompson are painting _____ living room.

4. I'm washing _____ hair.

6. We're washing _____ windows.

D. SHORT ANSWERS

Yes, I am.	Yes, $\left.\begin{array}{l}\text{he}\\\text{she}\\\text{it}\end{array}\right\}$ is.	Yes, $\left.\begin{array}{l}\text{we}\\\text{you}\\\text{they}\end{array}\right\}$ are.

1. Is Peggy fixing her car?

   Yes, _she_ _is._

2. Are you painting your living room?

   _____ _____ _____

3. Are your children cooking breakfast?

   _____ _____ _____

4. Are you and John cleaning the garage?

   _____ _____ _____

5. Is Michael feeding his cat?

   _____ _____ _____

6. Am I doing my homework?

   _____ _____ _____

7. Are Carol and Dan washing their clothes?

   _____ _____ _____

8. Is Mrs. McDonald doing her exercises?

   _____ _____ _____

16

E. WHAT ARE THEY DOING?

1. He's _____*feeding*_____

   his _____*dog*_____.

2. They're _____

   their _____.

3. He's _____

   his _____.

4. She's _____

   her _____ _____.

5. He's _____

   his _____.

6. He's _____

   his _____.

F. WHAT'S THE WORD?   Put a circle around the correct word.

1. ⬚ (Where) / We're ⬚ are you and Betty?

2. ⬚ Where / We're ⬚ in ⬚ our / are ⬚ room.

3. What are you doing?

   We're ⬚ washing / watching ⬚ TV.

4. ⬚ Is / His ⬚ Sam busy?

5. Yes, he is. ⬚ He's / His ⬚ cleaning ⬚ he's / his ⬚ room.

6. ⬚ Are / Our ⬚ Jane and Mark busy?

7. Yes, they are. ⬚ They're / Their ⬚ fixing ⬚ they're / their ⬚ car.

8. Where's the dog?

   ⬚ It's / Its ⬚ in the kitchen. ⬚ It's / Its ⬚ eating ⬚ its / it's ⬚ breakfast.

G. A BUSY DAY IN ROCKVILLE

bar	fixing	what's	his	Mr.	clothes
restaurant	playing	where's	her	Mrs.	newspaper
library	studying	they're	are	Miss	bicycle
laundromat					

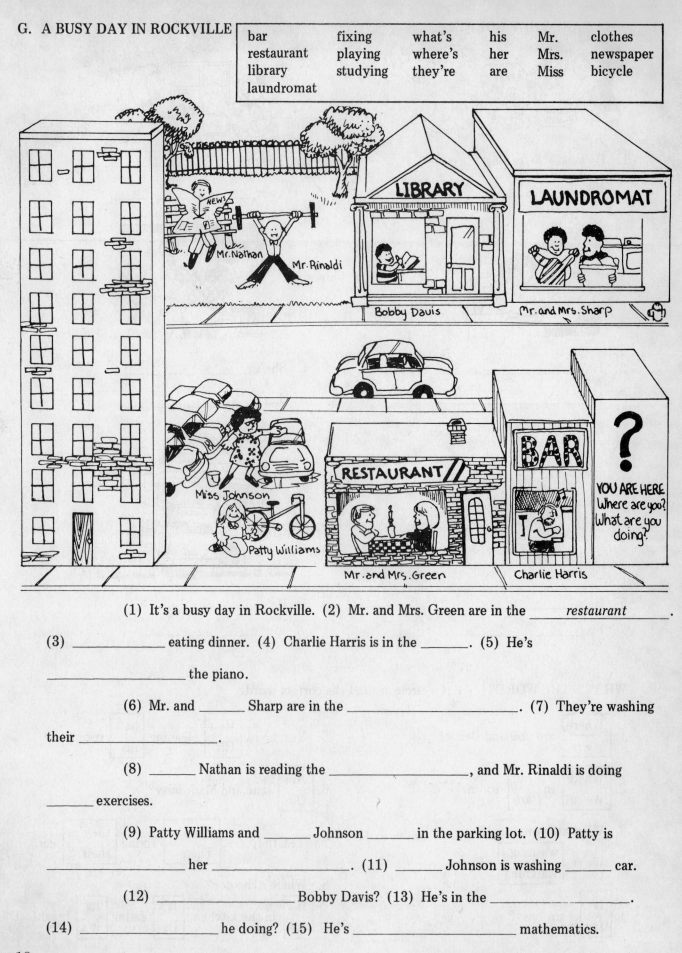

(1) It's a busy day in Rockville. (2) Mr. and Mrs. Green are in the _____ *restaurant* _____ .

(3) _____ eating dinner. (4) Charlie Harris is in the _____. (5) He's

_____ the piano.

(6) Mr. and _____ Sharp are in the _____. (7) They're washing

their _____.

(8) _____ Nathan is reading the _____, and Mr. Rinaldi is doing

_____ exercises.

(9) Patty Williams and _____ Johnson _____ in the parking lot. (10) Patty is

_____ her _____. (11) _____ Johnson is washing _____ car.

(12) _____ Bobby Davis? (13) He's in the _____.

(14) _____ he doing? (15) He's _____ mathematics.

18

OPPOSITES

A.   MATCHING OPPOSITES

Write the correct letter in the blank.

_f_	1. tall	a.	thin
____	2. heavy	b.	ugly
____	3. handsome	c.	single
____	4. rich	d.	cheap
____	5. married	e.	poor
____	6. easy	f.	short
____	7. expensive	'g.	old
____	8. young	h.	noisy
____	9. large	i.	difficult
____	10. quiet	j.	small

B.   WHAT ARE THEY SAYING?

Tell me about your new friend.

1. Is he rich or _____ _poor_ _____?

2. Is he tall or _____?

3. Is he heavy or _____?

4. Is he young or _____?

5. Is he handsome or _____?

6. Is he single or _____?

Tell me about your apartment.

7. Is it large or _____?

8. Is it noisy or _____?

9. Is it expensive or _____?

C. WHAT'S WRONG?

Correct the sentences.

He She It } isn't.	They aren't.

1. He's quiet.

He isn't quiet.

He's noisy.

2. It's cheap.

_____

_____

3. He's thin.

_____

_____

4. She's ugly.

_____

_____

5. He's short.

_____

_____

6. They're young.

_____

_____

D. SCRAMBLED QUESTIONS

Unscramble the questions. Begin each question with a capital letter.

1. _Is_ _English_ _difficult_ ?

difficult English is

2. _____ _____ _____?

tall are you

3. _____ _____ _____?

they are rich

4. _____ _____ _____

_____?

apartment your large is

5. _____ _____?

I beautiful am

6. _____ _____ _____ _____?

rich or poor she is

7. _____ _____

_____?

neighbors are noisy your

8. _____ _____ _____

_____?

John Mary and married are

20

E. MARGARET'S PHOTOGRAPHS

Label the photographs.

bicycle	cat	house
boss	dog	piano
car	guitar	sink

1. Helen: _Helen's_   _car_

2. Judy:_____ _____

3. Mr. and Mrs. Pepper:_____ _____ _____

_____ _____

4. Patty:_____ _____

5. Michael:_____ _____

6. John:_____ _____

7. Mr. Sharp:_____ _____ _____

8. Peter:_____ _____

9. Jim:_____ _____

F. WHAT'S THE WORD?

his	their
her	its

(John's)   1. ____*His*____ sister is married.

(Judy's)   2. _____ apartment is small.

(Fred and Sally's)   3. _____ dog is noisy.

(Miss Green's)   4. _____ car is new.

(Mr. and Mrs. Brown's) 5. _____ restaurant is cheap.

(Sam's)   6. _____ neighbors are quiet.

(Barbara's)   7. _____ brother is handsome.

(Mr. Larson's)   8. _____ cat is ugly.

(The dog's)   9. _____ name is Fido.

G. MEET FRED MCQUEEN

	I	am.
Yes,	he she it }	is.
	we you they }	are.

	I'm	not.
No,	he she it }	isn't.
	we you they }	aren't.

Fred McQueen is tall and handsome. He isn't fat, and he isn't thin. He's very rich.

Fred's car is new and beautiful. His house is large and expensive. His neighbors are rich and quiet. Fred isn't married.

1. Is Fred tall?   *Yes,*   *he*   *is.*

2. Is he short?   _____ _____ _____

3. Is he fat?   _____ _____ _____

4. Is he thin?   _____ _____ _____

5. Is he handsome?   _____ _____ _____

6. Is he poor?   _____ _____ _____

7. Is Fred's car new? _____ _____

8. Is it ugly?   _____ _____ _____

9. Is his house small? _____ _____ _____

10. Is it cheap?   _____ _____ _____

11. Are his neighbors rich? _____ _____ _____

12. Are they noisy?   _____ _____ _____

13. Is Fred single?   _____ _____ _____

22

H. WRITING CHECKS

Complete the checks with the correct information.

0	zero
1	one
2	two
3	three
4	four
5	five
6	six
7	seven
8	eight
9	nine
10	ten
11	eleven
12	twelve
13	thirteen
14	fourteen
15	fifteen
16	sixteen
17	seventeen
18	eighteen
19	nineteen
20	twenty
21	twenty-one
22	twenty-two
23	twenty-three
24	twenty-four
25	twenty-five
26	twenty-six
27	twenty-seven
28	twenty-eight
29	twenty-nine
30	thirty
40	forty
50	fifty
60	sixty
70	seventy
80	eighty
90	ninety
100	one hundred

1.

June 17, 19 *82*

PAY TO THE
ORDER OF *Johnson's Supermarket* $ *36.00*

Thirty-six and °°/100 DOLLARS

CENTRAL BANK
OHIO *Peter Nathan*

2.

February 5, 19 *83*

PAY TO THE
ORDER OF *City Hospital* $ *99.00*

and °°/100 DOLLARS

CENTRAL BANK
OHIO *Nancy Harris*

3.

January 10, 19 *83*

PAY TO THE
ORDER OF *Wilson's Supermarket* $ *48.00*

and °°/100 DOLLARS

CENTRAL BANK
OHIO *Albert Franklin*

4.

_____ 19 _____

PAY TO THE
ORDER OF _____ $ _____

_____ DOLLARS

CENTRAL BANK _____
OHIO

5.

_____ 19 _____

PAY TO THE
ORDER OF _____ $ _____

_____ DOLLARS

CENTRAL BANK _____
OHIO

23

I. LISTEN

Listen to the addresses of buildings. Fill in the correct numbers on the buildings.

J. THE WEATHER

it's sunny	it's warm	it's cold	it's raining
it's cloudy	it's cool	it's hot	it's snowing

Tokyo 100°F / 38°C

Madrid 70°F / 21°C

London 50°F / 10°C

Boston 32°F / 0°C

San Juan Mexico City Hong Kong Warsaw

1. How's the weather in Tokyo? *It's* _____ *sunny.*

2. How's the weather in London? _____ _____

3. How's the weather in Mexico City? _____ _____

4. How's the weather in Warsaw? _____ _____

5. How's the weather in Hong Kong? _____ _____

6. How's the weather in Madrid? _____ _____

7. How's the weather in San Juan? _____ _____

8. How's the weather in Boston? _____ _____

9. How's the weather in your city? ....

K. LISTEN

Listen to the temperature in Fahrenheit and Celsius. Write the numbers you hear.

1. Moscow *34°* F/ *1°* C   5. Paris _____ F/_____ C

2. Cairo _____ F/_____ C   6. Athens _____ F/_____ C

3. Caracas _____ F/_____ C   7. Tokyo _____ F/_____ C

4. San Francisco _____ F/_____ C   8. Rio de Janeiro _____ F/_____ C

25

A.   OUR FAMILY

husband
wife

Ted   Jane
Ted and Jane are married.

1. Ted is Jane's _____ *husband.* _____

2. Jane is Ted's _____ .

grandfather
grandmother
grandson
granddaughter

Fred   Hilda

father
mother
son
daughter
brother
sister

Ted   Jane

Bobby   Nancy

Bobby   Nancy

3. Bobby is Ted and Jane's _____ .

4. Nancy is their _____ .

5. Jane is Bobby and Nancy's

    _____ .

6. Ted is their _____ .

7. Bobby is Nancy's _____ .

8. Nancy is Bobby's _____ .

9. Hilda is Bobby and Nancy's

    _____ .

10. Fred is their _____ .

11. Bobby is Fred and Hilda's

    _____ .

12. Nancy is their _____ .

26

B. WHERE ARE THEY? WHAT ARE THEY DOING?

sitting	in front of	beach
standing		bench
swimming		

1. They're _____
   on the sofa.

2. He's at the _____.

3. She's _____.

4. She's _____.

5. They're _____
   the fireplace.

6. She's sitting on the

   _____.

C. OUT OF PLACE   Circle the word that doesn't belong.

1. car: garage, fixing, (cooking,) washing

2. beach: swimming, sink, hot, sunny

3. park: birds, bench, bank, soccer

4. living room: fireplace, television, sink, sofa

5. birthday party: sleeping, singing, dancing, eating

6. family: daughter, mother, neighbor, son

7. apartment: living room, bedroom,
   kitchen, classroom

8. weather: cloudy, short, raining, cool

9. eating: breakfast, newspaper,
   lunch, dinner

10. drinking: tea, birds, champagne, coffee

11. playing: guitar, baseball, piano, car

12. Bob: pretty, rich, tall, handsome

13. house: expensive, quiet, fat, beautiful

14. children: young, noisy, small, cloudy

27

D. A LETTER FROM NEW YORK CITY

Friday, June 10

Dear Walter,

We're on vacation in New York City, and we're having a good time. New York is beautiful. The weather is hot and sunny. It's 80°F.

Today my mother and father are at the Statue of Liberty. My sister Julie is swimming at the beach, and my brother Henry and his friends are playing soccer in the park.

I'm in Aunt Martha and Uncle Charlie's apartment. It's large and beautiful. Aunt Martha is cooking a big dinner, and Uncle Charlie is singing and playing the guitar.

Cousin Tommy and Cousin Gloria aren't on vacation. They're doing their homework in front of the TV. Their homework isn't easy.

How is the weather in Los Angeles? Is it hot?

What are you and your family doing? Are you busy studying?

See you soon,
Cousin Michael

E. Answer the questions in complete sentences.

1. How's the weather in New York City? _____ *It's hot and sunny.* _____

2. What's the temperature in New York? _____

3. Where are Michael's mother and father? _____

4. Who is Julie? _____

5. Where is she? _____

6. What's she doing? _____

7. Who is Henry? _____

8. Where is he? _____

9. What's he doing? _____

10. Where's Michael? _____

11. What's Aunt Martha doing? _____

12. Who is Charlie? _____

13. What's he doing? _____

14. Where are Tommy and Gloria? _____

15. What are they doing? _____

16. Who is Walter? _____

28

CHECK-UP TEST: Chapters 4-6

A. Put a circle around the correct answer.

Example: The children are noisy. They're

reading
sleeping
(singing) .

1. Bob is standing
   in
   on
   at
   front of the fireplace.

2. Rita is swimming at the
   beach
   bench
   bank
   .

3. Jane is
   brushing
   painting
   washing
   her teeth.

4. Peter is doing his
   sink
   homework
   room
   .

5. Michael is in the kitchen. He's
   fixing the
   sofa
   sink
   bed
   .

6. Betty is sitting on the
   sofa
   TV
   apartment
   .

7. Are you married? Yes, I
   is
   am
   are
   .

8. Are your neighbors rich? No,
   we
   you
   they
   aren't.

9. The cat is eating
   its
   it's
   he's
   dinner.

10. Where's Mr. Smith's car?
    His
    Her
    Its
    car is in the garage.

11. Where are Mrs. Johnson's neighbors?
    His
    Her
    Their
    neighbors are in the park.

12. Where's Mr. and Mrs. Brown's dog?
    Her
    His
    Their
    dog is in the bedroom.

13.
    Who
    Where
    What
    is he? He's my father.

14. My mother's mother is my
    aunt
    sister
    grandmother
    .

15. Is your house large?
    No,
    their
    her
    our
    house is small.

B. Write a sentence with the opposite adjective.

Ex. My apartment isn't large. _____It's small.____

1. Mr. and Mrs. Smith aren't quiet.

   _____

2. My husband isn't ugly. _____

3. We aren't heavy. _____

4. Miss Jones isn't young. _____

5. English isn't difficult. _____

C. Write the question.

Ex._____Is she ugly?_____ No, she isn't. She's beautiful.

1._____? No, it isn't. It's hot.

2._____? No, he isn't. He's short.

3._____? No, I'm not. I'm poor.

4._____? No, they aren't. They're expensive.

5._____? No, we aren't. We're single.

29

A. WHERE IS IT?

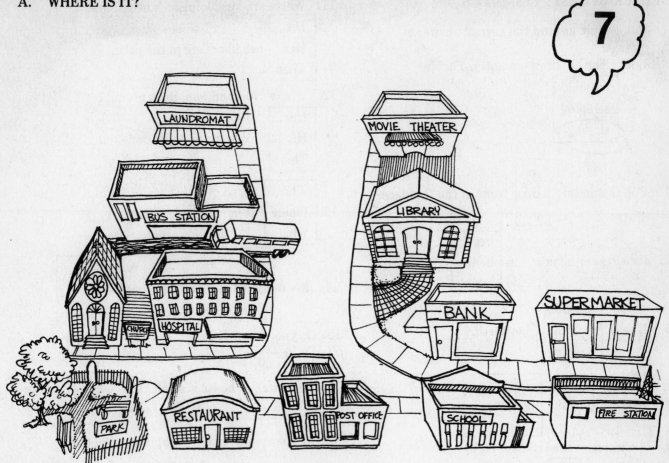

across from	around the corner from	between	next to

1. The park is _____*next to*_____ the restaurant.

2. The school is _____ the fire station.

3. The fire station is _____ the supermarket.

4. The post office is _____ the restaurant and the school.

5. The bank is _____ the library.

6. The supermarket is _____ the bank.

7. The restaurant is _____ the park and the post office.

8. The laundromat is _____ the movie theater.

9. The church is _____ the hospital.

10. The bus station is _____ the hospital.

B. WHAT ARE THEY SAYING?

1. Excuse me. Is there a library in this neighborhood?

   Yes, there is. ___There's___ a library on Main Street,

   ___across from___ the school.

2. Excuse me. _____ a hospital in this neighborhood?

   Yes, there is. _____ a hospital

   on State Street, _____ the park.

3. Excuse me. Is there a movie theater in this neighborhood?

   Yes, _____. _____

   a movie theater on Central Avenue,

   _____

   the bank.

4. Excuse me. _____ a church nearby?

   Yes, there is. _____ a church on State Street,

   _____

   the library and the _____.

5. Excuse me. _____ a post office in this neighborhood?

   Yes, _____. _____ a post office

   on _____ Street, _____ the laundromat.

31

C. LISTEN

Listen to these sentences about the buildings on the map. After each sentence write the name on the correct building.

1. fire station
2. police station
3. gas station
4. train station
5. school
6. drugstore
7. church
8. cafeteria
9. restaurant
10. movie theater
11. bank
12. post office
13. supermarket
14. library

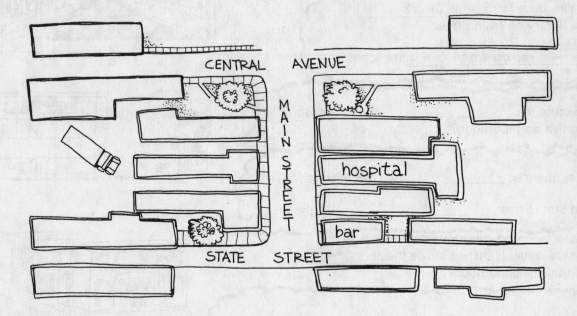

D. YES OR NO

Look at the map and answer the questions.

> Yes, there is.
> No, there isn't.

1. Is there a gas station on Main Street? _____ *Yes, there is.* _____

2. Is there a movie theater across from the train station? _____

3. Is there a supermarket around the corner from the drugstore? _____

4. Is there a post office across from the library? _____

5. Is there a school between the church and the fire station? _____

6. Is there a bank across from the movie theater? _____

7. Is there a police station next to the bar? _____

8. Is there a restaurant on Central Avenue? _____

9. Is there a hospital between the church and the fire station? _____

10. Is there a church next to the bank? _____

E. OUR APARTMENT BUILDING

broken	mice	roof
closet	pets	stove
fire escape	radiators	superintendent
mailbox		

1. There's a TV antenna on the _____roof._____

2. There's a _____ in the kitchen across from the sink.

3. There are _____ in the bedroom and living room. They're hot.

4. There's a _____ next to the bathroom.

5. There are two _____ in the building: a cat and a dog.

6. There aren't any clothes in the _____ in the bedroom.

7. There's a _____ between the building and the bus stop.

8. There are two _____ in the basement.

9. The _____'s apartment is in the basement.

10. There's a _____ window in the living room.

F. BARBARA'S LIVING ROOM

Yes, there is.	Yes, there are.
No, there isn't.	No, there aren't.

1. Is there a TV in Barbara's living room? _____ *Yes, there is.* _____

2. Is there a fireplace in Barbara's living room? _____

3. Are there any windows? _____

4. Are there any books on the TV? _____

5. Are there any clothes in the closet? _____

6. Is there a dog in front of the fireplace? _____

7. Is there a cat in the closet? _____

8. Are there any photographs on the piano? _____

9. Are there any cards on the sofa? _____

10. Are there any pets in Barbara's living room? _____

11. Is there a closet next to the fireplace? _____

12. Is there a newspaper in the closet? _____

13. Is there a guitar on the sofa? _____

14. How many books are there on the sofa? _____

15. How many photographs are there on the piano? _____

16. How many pets are there in the room? _____

17. How many cards are there on the piano? _____

18. How many windows are there in the room? _____

G.   LOOKING FOR AN APARTMENT

apt. = apartment	dinrm. = dining room	livrm. = living room
bath(s). = bathroom(s)	elev. = elevator	nr. = near
bdrm(s). = bedroom(s)	frpl(s). = fireplace(s)	rm(s). = room(s)
beaut. = beautiful	kit. = kitchen	schl. = school
bldg. = building	lge. = large	

DETROIT, quiet, sunny apt., kit., livrm., bdrm., bath., 2 frpls., nr. bus., no children. $500. 492-5683.

1. The apartment is in _____Detroit._____

2. It's quiet and _____.

3. There's a kitchen, a living room, a _____, and a _____.

4. There are two _____ in the apartment.

5. There aren't any _____ in the building.

BOSTON, sunny, lge. apt., kit., livrm., dinrm., 2 bdrms., bath., frpl., nr. schl., no pets. $800. 666-1700.

6. The apartment is in _____.

7. It's sunny and _____.

8. There are two _____ in the apartment.

9. _____ a fireplace in the apartment.

10. There's a _____ near the building.

11. There _____ any pets in the building.

LOS ANGELES, beaut., new apt., kit., livrm., 3 bdrms., 2 baths., elev. in bldg. $600. 715-8362.

12. The apartment is in _____.

13. It's _____ and new.

14. _____ _____ three _____ in the apartment.

15. There's an elevator in the _____.

A. WHAT ARE THEY WEARING?

belt	coat	jacket	raincoat	stocking
blouse	dress	mitten	shirt	suit
boot	earring	necklace	shoe	sweater
bracelet	glasses	pants	skirt	tie
briefcase	glasses	pocketbook	sock	umbrella
	hat			watch

1. _____hat_____
2. _____
3. _____
4. _____
5. _____
6. _____
7. _____
8. _____
9. _____
10. _____

11. _____
12. _____
13. _____
14. _____
15. _____
16. _____

17. _____
18. _____
19. _____
20. _____

21. _____
22. _____
23. _____
24. _____

36

25. _____

26. _____

27. _____

B. A/AN

1. __*a*__ bank

2. _____ school

3. _____ umbrella

4. _____ radio

5. _____ office

6. _____ post office

7. _____ hospital

8. _____ antenna

9. _____ elevator

10. _____ yard

11. _____ beach

12. _____ airport

13. _____ island

14. _____ house

15. _____ apartment

16. _____ library

17. _____ window

18. _____ aunt

19. _____ uncle

20. _____ neighbor

21. _____ hole

22. _____ earring

23. _____ woman

24. _____ exercise

C. SINGULAR/PLURAL

1. a hat / *hats*

2. __*a*__ ____*glove*____ / gloves

3. _____ _____ / sweaters

4. a necklace / _____

5. a tie / _____

6. a dress / _____

7. _____ _____ / classes

8. a watch / _____

9. _____ _____ / beaches

10. a bench / _____

11. a church / _____

12. an exercise / _____

13. _____ _____ / men

14. a woman / _____

15. _____ _____ / children

16. a mouse / _____

17. _____ _____ / teeth

18. _____ _____ / people

37

D. LISTEN

Listen to each word. Put a circle around the word you hear.

1. coat   (coats)   9. necklace   necklaces
2. car   cars   10. earring   earrings
3. umbrella   umbrellas   11. belt   belts
4. exercise   exercises   12. watch   watches
5. dog   dogs   13. bank   banks
6. shoe   shoes   14. house   houses
7. dress   dresses   15. jacket   jackets
8. restaurant   restaurants   16. glove   gloves

E. COLORS

Write sentences about yourself using colors.

red	orange	yellow	green	blue	purple
black	brown	pink	gray	white	gold
silver					

1. My house/apartment building is ....
2. My bedroom is . . . .
3. My kitchen is . . . .
4. My classroom is . . . .
5. My English book is . . . .
6. My shoes are . . . .

7. My socks/stockings are . . . .
8. My coat is . . . .
9. My hat is . . . .
10. My teeth are . . . .
11. My classroom is . . . .
12. My . . . . (is/are) . . . .

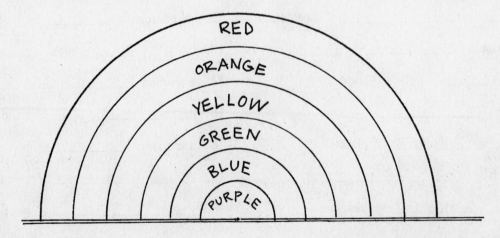

38

F.   WHAT'S IN MR. AND MRS. JACKSON'S CLOSET?

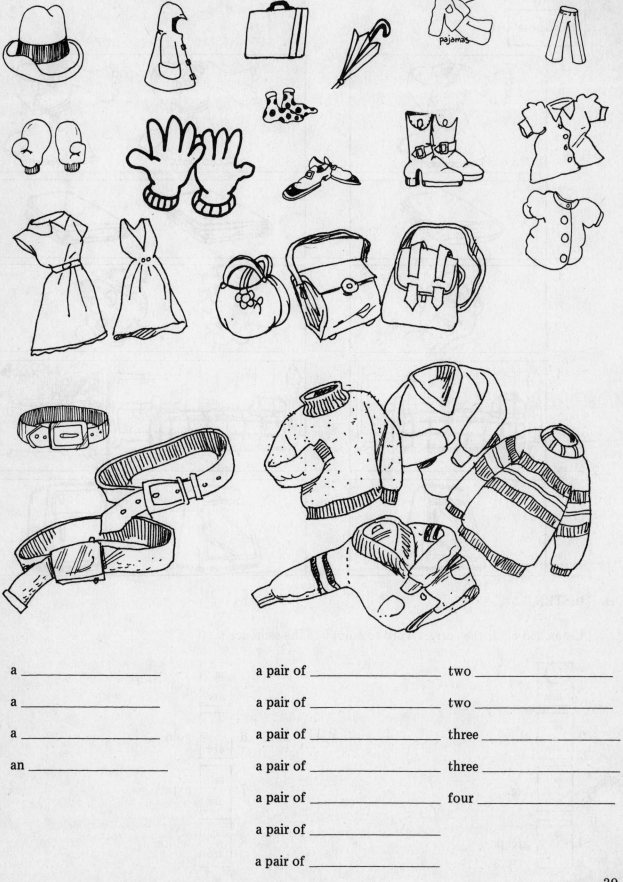

pajamas

a _____   a pair of _____   two _____

a _____   a pair of _____   two _____

a _____   a pair of _____   three _____

an _____   a pair of _____   three _____

                        a pair of _____   four _____

                        a pair of _____

                        a pair of _____

G. **LISTEN**

Listen to each sentence. Put a check (√) next to the appropriate picture.

this/these

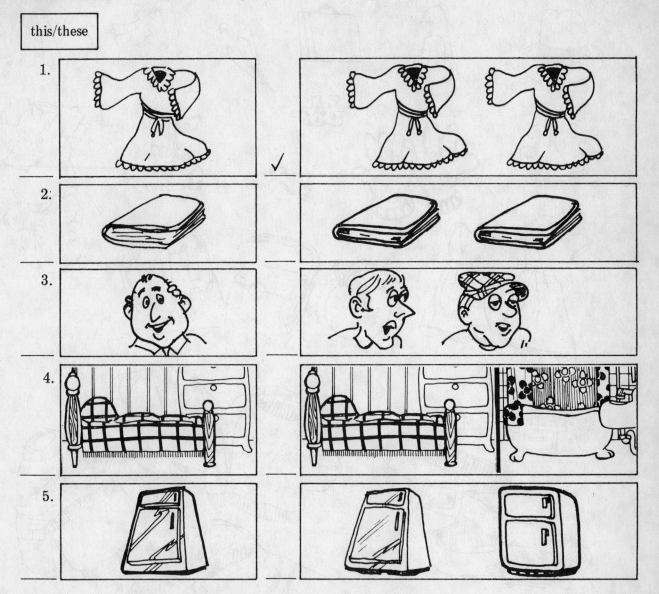

H. **LISTEN**

Listen and circle the correct word to complete the sentence.

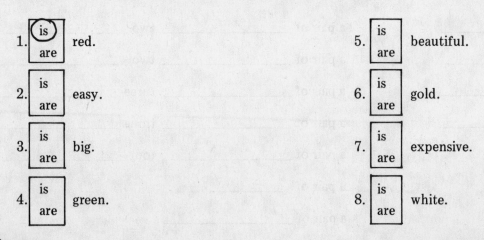

1. ⃝is / are red.

2. is / are easy.

3. is / are big.

4. is / are green.

5. is / are beautiful.

6. is / are gold.

7. is / are expensive.

8. is / are white.

I.   ALICE'S PHOTOGRAPH

this
these

Alice   Betty

that
those

Alice: _____*This*_____ is my favorite photograph. _____ is my mother, and _____ are my sisters.

Betty: _____*That*_____'s a beautiful photograph. Is _____ your brother?

Alice: Yes, it is, and _____ is my uncle.

Betty: Are _____ your cousins?

Alice: No, _____ are my brother's friends.

Betty: Who are _____ handsome men?

Alice: _____ are my neighbors, and _____ is my dog Rover.

Betty: No it isn't. _____'s your cat.

Alice: I'm sorry. I made a mistake. Where are my glasses?

41

J.   THIS/THAT/THESE/THOSE

this
these
that
those

blue   red

1. _____*This book is blue.*_____   2. _____*That book is red.*_____

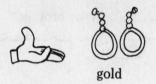

gold   silver

3. _____   4. _____

green   purple

5. _____   6. _____

small   big

7. _____   8. _____

cheap   expensive

9. _____   10. _____

K. SINGULAR→PLURAL

Write the sentences in the plural.

1. This hat is red. _____ *These hats are red.* _____

2. That skirt is short. _____

3. This watch is gold. _____

4. This necklace isn't expensive. _____

5. That dress is beautiful. _____

6. This woman is rich. _____

7. This is my child. _____

8. That isn't your pencil. _____

9. Is that your glove? _____

10. This isn't my sock. _____

L. PLURAL→SINGULAR

Write the sentences in the singular.

1. These bracelets are silver. _____ *This bracelet is silver.* _____

2. Those exercises are easy. _____

3. Are these your friends? _____

4. Are those your books? _____

5. These are Sally's blouses. _____

6. These men are my neighbors. _____

7. These aren't my mittens. _____

8. Those aren't my shoes. _____

9. Those churches are nearby. _____

10. Those are George's pets. _____

A.   Put a circle around the correct answer.

Ex.   My teeth are ⬭(white)⬭ .

> red
> **white**
> blue

1.   Jane is wearing a pair of ☐ .

> dresses
> blouses
> pants

2.   This ☐ is easy.

> questions
> homework
> exercises

3.   ☐ a church next to the bank.

> These
> They
> There's

4.   Is there a shirt on the bed?

No, ☐ .

> they isn't
> there isn't
> there aren't

5.   ☐ many rooms are there in the house?

> What
> Who
> How

6.   There's a ☐ on the sofa.

> woman
> umbrella
> earring

7.   There aren't any ☐ in the building.

> window
> pet
> children

B.   Put a circle around the word that doesn't belong.

Ex.   this, (their,) those, that, these

1.   green, yellow, silver, glove, gray

2.   blouse, shirt, sweater, coat, briefcase

3.   church, drugstore, fire escape, school, laundromat

4.   sister, brother, mother, house, father

C.   Answer the questions.

Ex.   Where's the post office?

It's around the corner from the hospital.

1.   Where's the restaurant?

_____

2.   Where's the school?

_____

3.   Where's the supermarket?

_____

D. Write sentences with *this*, *that*, *these*, and *those*.

yellow

Ex. _____ *These pencils are yellow.* _____

blue

1. _____

 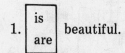

brown

2. _____

expensive

3. _____

E. Write the sentences in the plural.

Ex. This exercise is easy.

       These exercises are easy.

1. This dress is beautiful.

_____

2. That isn't my pen.

_____

3. Is that your briefcase?

_____

4. This watch isn't gold.

_____

F. LISTEN

Listen to the beginning of each sentence. Circle the correct word to complete the sentence.

Ex. | is |
    | are | white.

1. | is |
  | are | beautiful.

2. | is |
  | are | green.

3. | is |
  | are | new.

4. | is |
  | are | red.

A. INTERVIEWS AROUND THE WORLD

what	language	we	our	is	drink	read
what's	name	you	your	are	eat	sing
where	names	they	their	do	live	speak

1. ___*What's*___ your name?

2. My _____ _____ Mario.

3. Where _____ _____ live?

4. I _____ in Rome.

5. _____ _____ do you speak?

6. I _____ Italian.

7. What _____ _____ do every day?

8. Every day I _____ Italian food and I _____ Italian songs.

9. What _____ your names?

10. _____ _____ are Sara and Mark.

11. Where do _____ _____?

12. _____ _____ in London.

13. _____ language _____ _____ speak?

14. We _____ English.

15. What _____ you _____ every day?

16. Every day _____ _____ English beer and we _____ English newspapers.

17. _____ _____ their names?

18. _____ _____ _____
    Boris and Natasha.

19. _____ _____ they live?

20. _____ _____ _____ in Moscow.

21. _____ _____ _____ _____
    _____ _____ speak?

22. They _____ Russian.

23. What _____ they _____
    every day?

24. Every day _____ _____

    Russian food and _____

    _____ Russian tea.

B. PEOPLE AROUND THE WORLD

My name is Frank. I live in Montreal.
Every day I play the guitar and I
sing songs. I think music is
wonderful.

1. What's his name? _____ *His name is Frank.* _____

2. Where does he live? _____

3. What does he do every day? _____

My name is Robert. I live in Paris.
I speak French. Every day I read French books
and I listen to French music. I think French
is a wonderful language.

4. _____? His name is Robert.

5. _____? He lives in Paris.

6. What language does he speak? _____

7. What _____ every day? He _____ French books _____

   _____.

My name is Inga. I live in Stockholm.
I speak Swedish. Every day I do
exercises and I play soccer. I think
sports are wonderful.

8. What's her name? _____

9. _____ she live? _____

10. What language _____? She _____

11. _____ every day? She _____

   _____.

C. WRITE ABOUT YOURSELF

1. What's your name? ....

2. Where do you live? ....

3. What language do you speak? ....

4. What do you do every day? ....

   ....

48

D. MARIA'S FAMILY

Put a circle around the correct word.

(1) My name is Maria. (2) I ⓛive / lives in London. (3) I speak / speaks English and Spanish. (4) My

husband's name is John. (5) He speak / speaks English.

(6) Our children Fred and Sara speak / speaks English and Spanish. (7) At school they sing / sings English

and Spanish songs.

(8) We live / lives in a big house. (9) Every day I cook / cooks lunch and dinner, and I clean / cleans the

house. (10) Every day my husband cook / cooks breakfast, and he clean / cleans the yard. (11) We eat / eats big

English breakfasts and big Spanish dinners.

(12) Every day my husband and I read / reads the newspaper. (13) We drink / drinks tea and we listen / listens

to the radio. (14) I read / reads Spanish newspapers and my husband read / reads English newspapers.

(15) What do you do / does every day? (16) What languages do / does you speak?

E.   WRITE ABOUT MARIA'S FAMILY

1. Where does Maria live? _____ *She lives in London.* _____

2. What languages does she speak? _____

3. What language does Maria's husband speak? _____

4. What languages do Fred and Sara speak? _____

5. What do they do at school? _____

6. What does Maria do every day? _____

_____

_____

7. What does John do every day? _____

_____

_____

F.   LISTEN

Listen to the story. Write the missing words.

(1) Every day I sit in the park. (2) I _____ the newspaper, I _____ cards, I

_____ my lunch, and I _____ to the radio. (3) _____ not a busy person.

(4) My friend Harry _____ around the corner from my house. (5) Every day Harry

_____ his apartment, he _____ the piano, he _____ books, he _____

exercises, and he _____. (6) My friend Harry _____ a very busy person.

50

1. beach
2. bench
3. Charlie
4. children
5. Chinese
6. church

7. kitchen
8. teacher
9. watching
10. English
11. Natasha
12. Sharp

13. she's
14. shirt
15. shoes
16. station
17. washing
18. Washington

H. Fill in the words; then read the sentences aloud.

| beach | Charlie | Chinese |

1. ___*Charlie*___ is eating ___*Chinese*___

   food at the ___*beach*___.

| Natasha | station | Washington |

2. _____ is at the train _____

   in _____ D.C.

| children | kitchen | watching |

3. The _____ are _____ TV

   in the _____.

| Sharp | shirt | washing |

4. Mr. _____ is _____

   a _____.

| bench | church | teacher |

5. Our _____ is sitting on a _____

   in front of the _____.

| English | she's | shoes |

6. _____ wearing an _____ coat

   and English _____.

A. FRANKLIN'S INTERNATIONAL DISCOTHEQUE

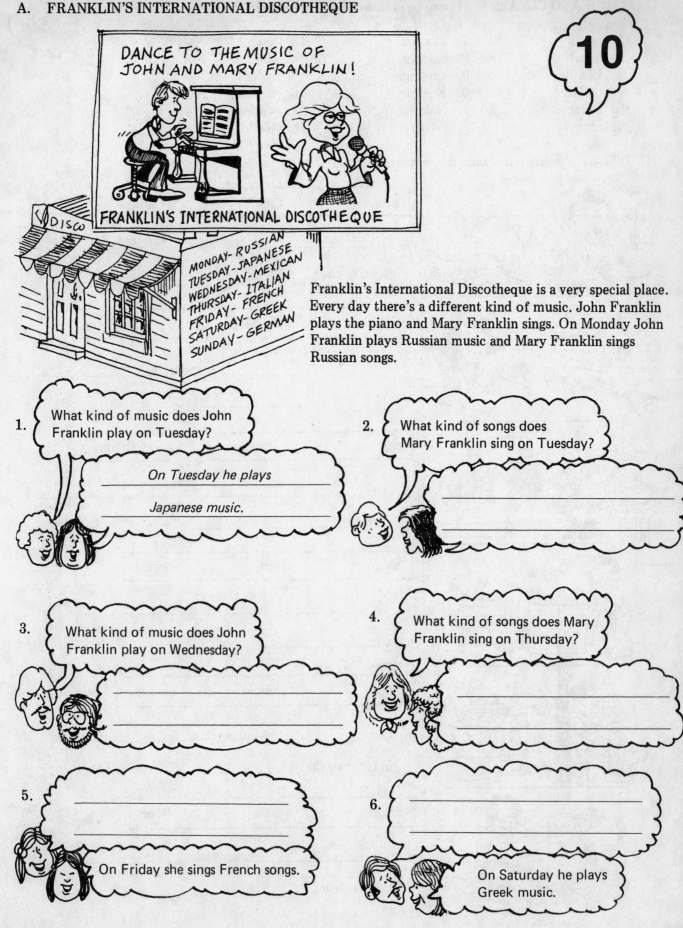

DANCE TO THE MUSIC OF JOHN AND MARY FRANKLIN!

10

FRANKLIN'S INTERNATIONAL DISCOTHEQUE

MONDAY - RUSSIAN
TUESDAY - JAPANESE
WEDNESDAY - MEXICAN
THURSDAY - ITALIAN
FRIDAY - FRENCH
SATURDAY - GREEK
SUNDAY - GERMAN

Franklin's International Discotheque is a very special place. Every day there's a different kind of music. John Franklin plays the piano and Mary Franklin sings. On Monday John Franklin plays Russian music and Mary Franklin sings Russian songs.

1. What kind of music does John Franklin play on Tuesday?

On Tuesday he plays

Japanese music.

2. What kind of songs does Mary Franklin sing on Tuesday?

_____

_____

3. What kind of music does John Franklin play on Wednesday?

_____

_____

4. What kind of songs does Mary Franklin sing on Thursday?

_____

_____

5. _____

_____

On Friday she sings French songs.

6. _____

_____

On Saturday he plays Greek music.

7. Does Mary Franklin sing Mexican songs on Wednesday?

Yes, she does.

8. Does John Franklin play Greek music on Thursday?

_____

9. _____

_____ on Sunday?

Yes, he does.

10. _____

_____ on Saturday?

No, she doesn't.

11. _____

_____ on Monday?

Yes, she does.

12. When does John Franklin play Mexican music?

He plays Mexican
music on Wednesday.

13. When does Mary Franklin sing French songs?

_____
_____

14. When does Mary Franklin sing Japanese songs?

_____
_____

15. When _____

_____ Italian music?

_____
_____

16. When _____

_____ Greek music?

_____
_____

17. When _____

_____ Mexican songs?

_____
_____

53

B. WHAT'S THE WORD?

do/does

1. What kind of books ___do___ you read?

2. _____ Margarita like American TV?

3. Why _____ Marie live in Tokyo?

4. Where _____ Mr. and Mrs. Smith play cards?

5. Why _____ Mrs. Wilson clean her house every day?

6. What _____ Mr. Wilson do every day?

7. _____ you like your new school? Yes, we _____.

8. When _____ Henry do his homework?

9. What kind of music _____ your mother and father listen to?

10. How many languages _____ you speak?

11. What kind of songs _____ you and your friends sing?

12.

_____ Tommy cry at the doctor's office?

Yes, he _____.

C. LISTEN

Listen to each question. Put a circle around the correct answer.

1. (a.) Mexican music.
   b. American food.
   c. Every day.

2. a. On Monday, Wednesday, and Friday.
   b. At school.
   c. Because they live in London.

3. a. Yes, he does.
   b. No, we don't.
   c. Yes, they do.

4. a. On Tuesday.
   b. We don't go there on Sunday.
   c. Because we like the clothes there.

5. a. He reads the newspaper.
   b. She plays cards.
   c. They feed the birds.

6. a. On Sunday.
   b. In Hong Kong.
   c. Because they like Chinese food.

7. a. On Friday.
   b. Across the street from the supermarket.
   c. Because she's rich.

8. a. He eats lunch.
   b. They play.
   c. Because it's hot.

9. a. No, she doesn't.
   b. No, we don't.
   c. Yes, they do.

10. a. He goes to the supermarket on Monday.
    b. We go to the supermarket on Tuesday.
    c. On Main Street.

54

D. YES AND NO

YES!

1. My grandfather drinks tea.

2. David and Tommy play baseball.

3. David's sister plays the guitar.

4. Albert and Walter drink lemonade.

5. Walter's father cleans the yard.

6. On Sunday we _____ to church.

7. Mr. and Mrs. Johnson _____ the newspaper.

8. Their children _____ TV.

9. The dog sleeps in the yard.

10. Peter's cat _____ mice.

11. I wear mittens to school.

12. My mother _____ stockings.

13. My sister feeds the dog.

14. On Saturday Mr. Johnson _____ to the beach.

15. Toshi speaks Japanese.

16. Margarita's cousin _____ in New York.

NO!

1. He _____doesn't_____ _____drink_____ beer.

2. They _____ _____ soccer.

3. She _____ _____ the piano.

4. They _____ _____ coffee.

5. He _____ _____ the apartment.

6. We don't go to school.

7. They don't read books.

8. They don't like homework.

9. It _____ _____ in the house.

10. It doesn't like children.

11. I _____ _____ gloves.

12. She doesn't wear socks.

13. She _____ _____ the cat.

14. He doesn't go to the library.

15. He _____ _____ Greek.

16. He doesn't live in San Juan.

E. WRITE ABOUT YOURSELF

YES!

1. I like ....

2. I play ....

3. I speak ....

4. I eat ....

5. I drink ....

NO!

1. I don't like ....

2. I don't play ....

3. I don't speak ....

4. I don't eat ....

5. I don't drink ....

55

F. A LETTER TO A PEN PAL   Read and practice.

Friday

Dear Paul,

My family and I live in Athens. We speak Greek. My mother is a music teacher. She plays the piano and sings. My father cooks at a restaurant.

My sister Helen and I go to a school near our house. We study history, Greek, science, mathematics, and English. My favorite school subject is history. I don't like mathematics and science, but I like languages.

Do you like sports? Every day at school I play soccer. On Saturday I play tennis. Which sports do you play?

What kind of music do you like? I think classical music is beautiful. I like jazz, but I don't like rock and roll.

What kind of movies do you like? I like American westerns and Italian comedies. I think war movies are terrible.

Tell me about your family and your school.

Your friend,
Anna

G. YOUR LETTER TO A PEN PAL

Dear . . . . ,

My family and I live in . . . . We speak

. . . .

At school I study . . . . , ... , and

. . . . My favorite subject is . . . .

I don't like . . . .

Which sports do you like? I play . . . . and

. . . . I think . . . . is wonderful. I don't

like . . . .

What kind of movies do you like? I like . . . .

very much, but I don't like . . . .

My favorite kind of music is . . . . , and I

like . . . . I don't listen to . . . .

Tell me about your school and your city.

Your friend,

. . . .

English
history
mathematics
music
science

baseball
football
golf
hockey
soccer
tennis

cartoons
comedies
dramas
science fiction
war movies
westerns

classical music
jazz
popular music
rock and roll

CHECK-UP TEST: Chapters 9-10

A. Put a circle around the correct answer.

Ex. I (like / likes) Japanese cars.

1. Mr. Jones (feed / feeds) the dog.

2. John and Mary (don't / doesn't) read at home.

3. Where (do / does) your sister live?

4. Mrs. Harris and her daughter (play / plays) baseball.

5. We (drink / drinks) Italian wine.

6. How many languages (do / does) Bob speak?

B. Fill in the blanks.

Ex. ___What___ is your name?

1. _____ do you live?

2. _____ kind of music do they like?

3. _____ does Paul go to the bank? On Friday.

4. _____ do you listen to the radio every day? Because we like music.

5. _____ Frank go to church on Sunday? Yes, he _____ .

6. _____ does Mrs. Smith do on Tuesday?

C. Fill in the blanks.

Mrs. Williams _____ in Miami.

She's old, but she _____ exercises every day. On Monday she _____ her apartment, on Wednesday she _____ cards, on Friday she _____ to music, and on Sunday she _____ the newspaper. She doesn't cook dinner on Sunday because she and her friends _____ to Stanley's International Restaurant. Mrs. Williams _____ Miami is a wonderful city.

D. LISTEN

Listen to each question. Put a circle around the correct answer.

Ex. a. French food.
  (b.) Italian songs.
  c. At the discotheque.

1. a. Yes, she does.
   b. No, they don't.
   c. Because they're young.

2. a. He feeds the birds.
   b. Because it's hot.
   c. On Sunday.

3. a. We study English.
   b. Every day.
   c. Yes, I do.

4. a. They like American music.
   b. He lives on Central Street.
   c. They live on Main Street.

5. a. On Saturday.
   b. Because we like the food.
   c. In Rome.

A. **WHAT ARE THEY SAYING?**

me	us
him	you
her	them
it	

1. Do you like me?
   Of course I like _you_.

2. Do you like Bob?
   Of course I like _____.

3. Do you like my new tie?
   Of course I like _____.

4. Do you like Fred and Martha?
   Of course I like _____.

5. Do you like Mary?
   Of course I like _____.

6. Does Mary like you?
   Of course she likes _____.

7. Of course he likes _____.
   Does the teacher like you?

8. Do you like discotheques?
   Of course I like _____.

58

9. Do you like your new apartment?

Of course I like _____.

10. Do you like your new neighbors?

Of course I like _____.

B. WRITE ABOUT YOURSELF

always	usually	sometimes	rarely	never

1. I .... *always* .... read the newspaper.

2. I .... eat breakfast.

3. I .... cook dinner.

4. I .... dance at parties.

5. I .... watch TV.

6. I .... do my homework.

7. I .... listen to American music.

8. I .... go to Italian restaurants.

9. I .... drink champagne at parties.

10. I always ....

11. I usually ....

12. I sometimes ....

13. I rarely ....

14. I never ....

C. WRITE AND SAY IT

Correct the word in parentheses and then say the sentence.

1. John never (feed) _____ *feeds* _____ his cat.

2. Nancy rarely (help) _____ her brother.

3. Judy always (fix) _____ her car.

4. Mrs. Smith rarely (talk) _____ to her husband.

5. Mary usually (brush) _____ her teeth.

6. My father sometimes (wash) _____ the clothes.

7. Linda never (go) _____ to school.

8. Tommy sometimes (dance) _____ with his sister.

9. When Jane (do) _____ her homework, she usually (eat) _____.

10. When my grandfather (watch) _____ TV, he always (sit) _____ on the sofa.

D. WHAT'S THE WORD?

it	her	him	them

1. I always talk to _____ *her.* _____

2. Why don't you listen to _____?

3. I read _____ on Sunday.

4. I dance with _____ when I go to the discotheque.

5. What do you feed _____?

6. Do you wash _____ every day?

E. LISTEN

Listen to each sentence. Put a check (√) next to the appropriate picture.

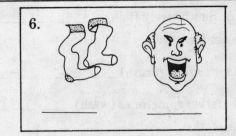

60

F. WHAT ARE THEY SAYING?

have	do	don't
has	does	doesn't

1. _____Does_____ Johnny _____have_____ any brothers?

No. He _____doesn't_____ _____have_____ any brothers, but he _____has_____ a big sister.

2. Do you have any French wine?

No. We _____ _____ any French wine, but we _____ Italian wine.

3. We're looking for our child. She _____ long brown hair.

What color eyes does she _____?

4. Do your children have a good teacher?

Yes. They _____ a wonderful teacher.

5. What kind of car _____ your brother _____?

He _____ a Toyota.

6. _____ they _____ any shirts?

No. They _____ _____ any shirts, but they _____ beautiful ties.

7. _____ your new apartment _____ a dining room?

Yes. It _____ a dining room and a big kitchen.

MY GRANDMOTHER

G.   LISTEN

Listen to the story. Write the missing words.

(1) My grandmother _has_ brown eyes and gray curly ____hair____. (2) She's short and

heavy. (3) She _____ with _____, and I'm very glad. (4) Here's why I _____

she's wonderful.

(5) When we _____ to parties, my grandmother always _____ with me. (6) When I

_____ to her, she always _____ to me, and when my friends talk to

_____, she listens to _____.

(7) When I have difficult homework, my grandmother usually _____ me. (8) When

I'm hungry, she always _____ _____. (9) When we _____ together, she

_____ _____ to me, and when I'm upset, she always _____ with _____.

(10) My grandmother is rarely upset. (11) When our clothes are dirty, she

_____ them. (12) When the sink is broken, she _____ it. (13) When my

little sisters are noisy, she _____ with _____.

(14) My grandmother is really wonderful.

H.   YES OR NO

Yes, she is.	No, she isn't.
Yes, she does.	No, she doesn't.

1.   Does my grandmother have brown eyes?   _____ _Yes, she does._ _____

2.   Does she have brown hair?   _____

3.   Is she tall?   _____

4.   Is she heavy?   _____

5.   Does she dance with me when we go to parties? _____

6.   Does she watch TV when we eat together?   _____

7.   Is she usually upset?   _____

8.   Does she listen to my friends when they talk to her? _____

9.   Is she lazy?   _____

10. Is she wonderful?   _____

62

I. A WONDERFUL PERSON

Write five sentences about a person you think is wonderful. Tell why.

1. ....

2. ....

3. ....

4. ....

5. ....

J. WHAT'S THE WORD?

Put a circle around the correct word.

1. Maria is listening (to) / at / with the radio.

2. My uncle always dances to / at / with me.

3. John is playing soccer to / at / with us.

4. My children never talk to / at / on me.

5. Do you live in / on / at Tokyo?

6. Tell me to / at / about your city.

7. The post office is in / on / between Main Street.

8. I always listen at / to / on the radio when I eat breakfast.

9. I'm having a wonderful time in / on / at my party.

10. Is there a refrigerator in / on / at the kitchen?

11. Do Paul and Robert go (to) / at / in school?

12. We're looking from / for / to a yellow umbrella.

13. The children are to / at / in the beach.

14. Natasha is wearing a pair of / from / for boots.

15. Alice is sitting in / on / with a bench in / on / with the park.

16. Martha goes to / at / in church in / on / at Sunday.

63

A. WHAT'S THE WORD?

angry	hot	sad
embarrassed	hungry	sick
happy	nervous	thirsty
		tired

12

1. Henry is wearing a suit at the beach.

He's _____ *hot* _____.

2. Alice is yawning. She's _____.

3. Mr. Smith's students never do their

homework. Mr. Smith is _____.

4. Robert made a mistake in class.

He's _____.

5. Gloria likes her new apartment.

She's _____.

6. Edward is drinking lemonade.

He's _____.

7. Walter's new car is broken.

He's _____.

8. Jane has an English test on Monday.

She's _____.

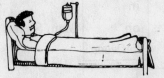

9. Paul is eating a big breakfast.

He's _____.

10. Peter is in the hospital.

He's _____.

64

B.   TELL ME WHY

1. Why is he smoking?

    He's smoking because he's nervous.

    He always ___*smokes when he's nervous.*___

2. Why are you yawning?

    _____ tired.

    I always _____ .

3. Why are they shouting?

    _____ angry.

    They always _____ .

4. Why are you shivering?

    _____ cold.

    We always _____ .

5. Why is he perspiring?

    _____ hot.

    He always _____ .

6. Why are they crying?

    _____ sad.

    They always _____ .

7. Why is he going to a restaurant?

    _____ hungry.

    He always _____ .

8. Why is she smiling?

    _____ happy.

    She always _____ .

9.

Why are you blushing?

_____ embarrassed.

I always _____ .

C. THAT'S STRANGE!

1. My sister is cooking dinner today.

That's strange! She never ___cooks___ dinner.

2. The children are studying English today.

That's strange! They never _____ English.

3. I'm cleaning my room today.

That's strange! You never _____ your room.

4. David is playing with his brother.

That's strange! He never _____ with his brother.

5. The cat _____ _____ in the garage today.

That's strange! It never sleeps in the garage.

6. Mr. and Mrs. Wilson _____ _____.

That's strange! They never dance.

7. Our mother _____ _____ the dishes today.

That's strange! She never _____ the dishes.

8. Our teacher _____ _____ today.

That's strange! She never smiles.

9. We're watching TV today.

That's strange! You never _____ TV.

10. Mr. and Mrs. Jones _____ _____ the newspaper today.

That's strange! They never read the newspaper.

11. Sally is helping her sisters today.

That's strange! She never _____ them.

12. My brother and I _____ _____ football today.

That's strange! You never play football.

13. My mother and father are shouting.

That's strange! They never _____.

14. I'm _____ coffee today.

That's strange! You never drink coffee.

15. My grandfather is listening to rock and roll music.

That's strange! He never _____ to rock and roll music.

D. WHAT'S THE QUESTION?

1. I'm crying because I'm sad. (Why?) _____ *Why are you crying?* _____

2. They play tennis in the park. (Where?) _____ *Where do they play tennis?* _____

3. She goes to the library on Wednesday. (When?) _____

_____

4. They're singing because they're happy. (Why?) _____

5. She's going to the beach. (Where?) _____

6. He washes his clothes at the laundromat. (Where?) _____

_____

7. I like German beer. (What kind of?) _____

8. She has ten grandchildren. (How many?) _____

9. He's eating at the cafeteria today. (Where?) _____

10. I'm wearing two sweaters. (How many?) _____

11. She's reading. (What?) _____

12. They play soccer on Tuesday. (What?) _____

13. He smokes French cigarettes. (What kind of?) _____

_____

14. We're cooking a big dinner because we're hungry. (Why?) _____

_____

E. LISTEN

As you listen to each story, read the following sentences and check <u>yes</u> or <u>no</u>. You will hear each story twice.

Jane and Betty

1. yes ☐ no ☑ Jane and Betty are looking for a discotheque.

2. yes ☐ no ☐ Jane and Betty are very angry.

3. yes ☐ no ☐ Their mother isn't cooking dinner today.

Am I Lazy?

4. yes ☐ no ☐ I always do my homework.

5. yes ☐ no ☐ I always help my mother in the kitchen.

6. yes ☐ no ☐ My mother thinks I'm lazy.

Tom

7. yes ☐ no ☐ Tom is usually happy.

8. yes ☐ no ☐ Tom is smiling today.

9. yes ☐ no ☐ Tom's sister is studying.

Vacation

10. yes ☐ no ☐ I like vacations.

11. yes ☐ no ☐ When it's hot, I read books and listen to music.

12. yes ☐ no ☐ My sister and I are playing tennis in the park.

F. LOUD AND CLEAR

Fill in the words; then read the sentences aloud.

Spanish	Steven	studying	what's

1. ___What's___ ___Steven___ doing?

He's ___studying___ ___Spanish___.

likes	smiling	Stanley	suit

2. _____ is

_____ because he

_____ his new _____.

68

Alice	boss	nervous	talks

3. _____ is _____

when she _____ to her

_____ .

bicycle	Stuart	school	sunny

4. When it's _____ , _____

goes to _____ on his

_____ .

Sam	sister	singing	sleeping	song

5. _____ isn't _____ because

his _____ is

_____ a loud _____ .

hospital	Mrs.	sick	sorry	Wilson

6. Mr. _____ is in the

_____ . _____ Wilson is

_____ he's _____

Boris	bus	next	school

7. _____ always sits _____ to

the _____ driver on the _____
bus.

asks	listen	science	students	question

8. When the _____ teacher

_____ a _____ ,

her _____ always

_____ .

69

CHECK-UP TEST: Chapters 11-12

A. Fill in the blanks.

me	him	her	it	us	you	them

Ex. Do you like Mr. Wilson?

Of course I like *him* .

1. Does John listen to his mother?

Of course he listens to _____ .

2. When the windows are dirty, I

always wash _____ .

3. I don't like TV, but I'm watching

_____ today.

4. Bob rarely plays with his brother,

but he's playing with _____ today.

5. When my sister and I are hungry, my

mother always feeds _____ .

B. Fill in the blanks.

Ex. I never eat breakfast, but I'm

_____ *eating* _____ breakfast today.

1. Mary never shouts, but she's

_____ today.

2. We never _____ to the library, but
we're going to the library today.

3. Mr. and Mrs. Jones never dance, but

they're _____ today.

4. John never _____ his car, but
he's fixing his car today.

5. Tommy never _____ the
dishes, but he's washing the dishes today.

C. Fill in the blanks.

do	does	is	are

Ex. a. What _____ *does* _____ Walter usually do
on Sunday?

b. Where _____ *is* _____ Bobby studying?

1. When _____ Mary and Walter usually go
to the bank?

2. Why _____ Barbara shivering?

3. _____ Bill usually wash the dishes?

4. _____ Jack and Judy cooking dinner today?

5. Do they have any pets? Yes, they

_____ .

D. Write the question.

Ex. I'm crying because I'm sad. (Why?)

_____ *Why are you crying?* _____

They play tennis in the park. (Where?)

_____ *Where do they play tennis?* _____

1. She goes to the supermarket on Wednesday.
(When?)

_____

2. He's yawning because he's tired. (Why?)

_____

3. They're sleeping on the floor. (Where?)

_____

4. She has three children. (How many?)

_____

5. I'm drinking coffee. (What?)

_____

E. LISTEN

Listen to each question. Put a circle around
the correct answer.

Ex. a. They're playing baseball.
b. They play tennis.

1. a. We're dancing.
b. We drink champagne.

2. a. I'm going to the beach.
b. I go to school.

3. a. He's smoking.
b. He eats.

4. a. She's cooking Italian food.
b. She cooks French food.

5. a. Yes, he is.
b. Yes, he does.

A. CAN OR CAN'T

cook	sing	speak
dance	skate	swim
play		

1. Harry *can't* *play* the piano.

   He *can* *play* *the* *guitar* .

2. We _____ _____ .

   We _____ _____ .

3. I _____ _____ chess.

   I _____ _____

   _____ .

4. Alice _____ _____ .

   She _____ _____ .

5. John and Robert _____

   _____ the violin.

   They _____ _____

   _____ .

6. Walter _____ _____
   Italian food.

   He _____ _____

   _____ .

7. Mary _____ _____ .

   She _____ _____ .

8. Hans _____ _____ German.

   He _____ _____ _____ .

71

B. WRITE ABOUT YOURSELF

What can you do?

1. I can ....·

2. ....

3. ....

4. ....

5. ....

What can't you do?

1. I can't..·

2. ....

3. ....

4. ....

5. ....

C. PUZZLE

What do they do for a living?

ACROSS

1. He drives a truck.
6. He bakes pies.
9. She acts on TV.

DOWN

1. He teaches in a school.
2. She fixes cars every day.
3. He dances every day.
4. She plays the violin.
5. She cooks in a restaurant.
7. He acts in the movies.
8. He sings every day.

D. LISTEN

Listen to each sentence. Put a circle around the word you hear.

1. (can)   can't
2. can   can't
3. can   can't
4. can   can't

5. can   can't
6. can   can't
7. can   can't
8. can   can't

9. can   can't
10. can   can't
11. can   can't
12. can   can't

72

E. WHAT'S THE QUESTION?

1. _____Can she bake ?_____ ?
   Yes, she can.

2. _____ ?
   No, he can't.

3. _____ ?
   Yes, they can.

4. _____ ?
   Yes, I can.

5. _____ ?
   No, they can't.

6. _____ ?
   Yes, he can.

F. THE NELSON FAMILY

Fill in the blanks.

Sally Nelson ___is___ an actress. She's young and pretty, but when she acts, she can look young or old, beautiful or _____, happy or _____.

Her husband Bob _____ an English _____. He teaches students from cities around the world. His students speak Spanish, French, Russian, and Arabic. Bob sometimes _____ Spanish and French with them, but he can't _____ Russian or Arabic.

Sally is a good athlete. She _____ tennis and golf very well. When it's cold she skis, and when it's _____ she swims _____ day.

Bob doesn't like sports. He can't _____ tennis or golf, but he _____ ski. When he isn't busy, he usually _____ the newspaper or _____ chess. He likes chess because he _____ play very well.

Sally and Bob both love music. Sally sings popular _____ and _____ the piano. Bob can't play the piano, but he _____ sing and he can _____ the violin.

have to	do	don't
has to	does	doesn't

1. Why are you upset?

I _have_ _to_ go to the dentist.

2. Why is Johnny angry?

He _____ _____ clean his room.

3. Do we _____ _____ go to the supermarket?

_____ you _____ work today?

4. No, I _____. I'm on vacation.

5. _____ I _____ _____ wear a sweater?

Of course you _____. It's very cold today.

6. Why is Franklin smiling?

He _____ _____ work on Friday.

74

H. A BUSY WEEK

Monday	Tuesday	Wednesday	Thursday
Tom: go to the supermarket Helen: wash the clothes	Tom and Helen : go to the dentist	Tom: clean the yard Helen: fix the car	Tom and Helen : paint the bedroom

Tom and Helen are very busy people.

1. What does Tom have to do on Monday? _____ *He has to go to the supermarket.* _____

2. What does Helen have to do on Wednesday? _____

3. What does Helen have to do on Monday? _____

4. What do Tom and Helen have to do on Thursday? _____

5. What do Tom and Helen have to do on Tuesday? _____

6. What does Tom have to do on Wednesday? _____

I. WRITE ABOUT YOURSELF

What do YOU have to do this week?

....

....

....

....

....

....

J. WE'RE BUSY

can't	do the laundry	go skiing	play cards
have to	fix the TV	go swimming	play tennis
has to	go dancing	go to the dentist	study
	go jogging	go to the doctor	teach
	go sailing	go to the zoo	wash the kitchen floor
			work

1. John _____ *can't go skiing* _____ today.

He _____ *has to study* _____.

2. Richard and Alice _____ today.

They _____.

3. Mrs. Smith _____ today.

She _____.

4. I _____ today.

I _____.

5. Paul _____ today.

He _____.

6. Mrs. Wilson _____ today.

She _____.

7. We _____ today.

We _____.

8. Mrs. Brown _____ today.

She _____.

76

A. WHAT ARE THEY GOING TO DO?

1. What's Sally going to do this afternoon?

   She's going to study English.

2. What are Mr. and Mrs. Green going to do tomorrow morning?

   _____

3. What's Helen going to do tomorrow afternoon?

   _____

4. What are you and George going to do this morning?

   _____

5. What's your grandfather going to do this evening?

   _____

6. What are Jane and her mother going to do today?

   _____

7. _____ Linda _____ tonight?

   _____

8. _____ you _____ this morning?

   _____

77

B. AN INTERNATIONAL MOVIE ACTOR

JANUARY - Rome
FEBRUARY - Geneva
APRIL - London
JUNE - Honolulu
SEPTEMBER - TOKYo

George Dupont is a famous international movie actor. He lives in Paris, but he always works in cities around the world.

Next January George is going to act in Rome. He's glad he's going to work there because he loves Italian music. In the evening when he isn't busy, he's going to go to concerts.

Next February George is going to go skiing in Geneva with his wife and son. George always goes skiing on his winter vacation, and he always has a wonderful time.

Next April George is going to work in London. His wife and son are going to visit him every weekend. When they're together, they're going to go shopping in expensive London stores, and his son is going to go to the London Zoo.

Next June George and his family are going to go to Honolulu on their summer vacation. They love the beautiful beaches there, and they're going to go swimming and sailing every day.

Next September George is going to go to Tokyo. He's going to act in a Japanese movie. His family can't go with him, but he isn't upset because his son and wife are going to write to him from Paris. When he isn't working, he's going to go to Japanese restaurants and baseball games with his friends.

1. When is George going to go to Rome? _____ *He's going to go to Rome next January.*

2. What's he going to do in Rome in the evening? _____

_____

3. When are George and his family going to go to Geneva? _____

_____

4. What are they going to do there? _____

_____

5. Where is George going to work next April? _____

6. What are George and his family going to do in London? _____

_____

7. When are George and his family going to go to Honolulu? _____

_____

8. What are they going to do there? _____

9. When is George going to go to Tokyo? _____

10. Why is George going to go to Tokyo? _____

11. What's he going to do there when he isn't working? _____

_____

C. WHAT'S THE QUESTION?

1. I'm going to <u>fix my car</u> this afternoon. (What?) *What are you going to do this afternoon?*

2. He's going to cut his hair <u>next week</u>. (When?) _____

3. They're going to go to <u>Madrid</u> next summer. (Where?)_____

   _____

4. She's going to plant flowers <u>this spring</u>. (When?)_____

5. He's going to visit his grandmother <u>because she's sick.</u> (Why?)_____

   _____

6. They're going to <u>write</u> to their brother this morning. (What?)_____

   _____

7. I'm going to call the plumber <u>right away</u>. (When?)_____

8. He's going to eat <u>at a restaurant</u> tonight. (Where?) _____

   _____

D. LISTEN

Listen to the following weather forecasts. Put a circle around the correct answer. You will hear each forecast twice.

TODAY'S WEATHER FORECAST

1. This afternoon:

   (warm)   cool   (sunny)   cloudy   rain

2. This evening:

   warm   cool   sunny   cloudy   rain

THIS WEEKEND'S FORECAST

3. Tonight:

   cool   cold   sunny   clear   foggy

4. Saturday:

   cool   cold   sunny   clear   foggy

5. Sunday:

   cool   cold   sunny   clear   foggy

MONDAY'S WEATHER FORECAST

6. Monday morning:

   cool   cold   sunny   cloudy   snow

7. Monday afternoon and evening:

   cool   cold   sunny   cloudy   snow

8. Tuesday:

   cool   cold   sunny   cloudy   snow

E. BAD WEATHER

go skating	paint the house	be cloudy
go to a baseball game	wash the car	be cold
go to the park		be warm
have a picnic		rain
		snow

1. What do Shirley and Patty want to do tomorrow?

   _____*They want to go skating.*_____

   What's the forecast?

   _____*It's going to be warm.*_____

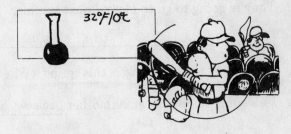

2. What does Jeff want to do tomorrow?

   _____

   What's the forecast?

   _____

3. What do Gloria and Frank want to do tomorrow?

   _____

   What's the forecast?

   _____

4. What does Lois want to do tomorrow?

   _____

   What's the forecast?

   _____

5. What do Anita and Ted want to do tomorrow?

   _____

   What's the forecast?

   _____

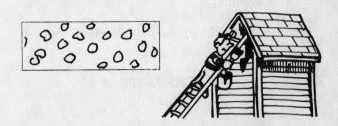

6. What does Sam want to do tomorrow?

   _____

   What's the forecast?

   _____

F. YES AND NO

YES!	NO!
1. John wants to play chess.	*He doesn't want to play* checkers.
2. Mary wants to go to the zoo.	_____ to a concert.
3. I want to visit my friend.	_____ my grandmother.
4. Mr. and Mrs. Smith want to eat dinner at a restaurant.	_____ dinner at home.
5. We want to study Arabic.	_____ mathematics.
6. Our English cousins want to drink tea.	_____ coffee.
7. Bob wants to dance with Lois.	_____ with his sister.

G. YES AND NO

I'm not
He
She } isn't
It

going to

We
You } aren't
They

YES!	NO!
1. Bill is going to call his uncle.	*He isn't going to call* his mother.
2. I'm going to fix the TV.	_____ the sink.
3. We're going to go skating.	_____ skiing.
4. My aunt and uncle are going to live in London.	_____ in Berlin.
5. Mr. Jones is going to listen to music.	_____ to the forecast.
6. It's going to be cloudy.	_____ sunny.
7. Alice is going to cook dinner.	_____ lunch.

81

H. FUTURE HOPES

Sally is a mechanic, but she wants to be a teacher. She wants to teach English in Mexico City.

1. _____What_____ _____does_____ Sally _____want_____ __to__ be?

   _She__ _____wants_____ _____to_____ __be__ a teacher.

2. _____ _____ she _____ _____ teach?

   _____ _____ _____ English.

3. _____ _____ she _____ _____ work?

   _____ _____ _____ _____ in Mexico City.

Arthur is a teacher, but he wants to be a mechanic. He wants to work in a garage and fix cars.

4. _____ _____ Arthur _____ _____ be?

   _____ _____ _____ _____ a mechanic.

5. _____ _____ he _____ _____ do?

   _____ _____ _____ fix cars.

6. _____ _____ he _____ _____ work?

   _____ _____ _____ _____ in a garage.

I. WRITE ABOUT YOURSELF

What do you want to be? What do you want to do? Where do you want to work?

....

....

....

....

....

82

J. WHAT TIME IS IT?

Draw the time on the clocks.

2:00

It's two o'clock.

2:15

It's two fifteen.
It's a quarter after two.

2:30

It's two thirty.
It's half past two.

2:45

It's two forty-five.
It's a quarter to three.

12:00

It's twelve o'clock.
It's noon.

12:00

It's twelve o'clock.
It's midnight.

1. It's three o'clock.

2. It's one fifteen.

3. It's four thirty.

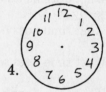
4. It's seven forty-five.

5. It's five thirty.

6. It's nine forty-five.

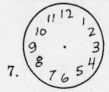
7. It's noon.

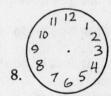
8. It's six fifteen.

9. It's ten thirty.

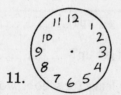
10. It's a quarter after five.

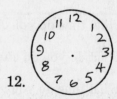
11. It's half past eleven.

12. It's a quarter to eight.

K. LISTEN

Listen and write the time you hear.

1. _____9:30_____

2. _____

3. _____

4. _____

5. _____

6. _____

7. _____

8. _____

9. _____

10. _____

11. _____

12. _____

83

L. PAUL SMITH'S DAY

   Paul Smith gets up every day at 8:00. He takes a bath and reads the newspaper. At 8:30 he eats breakfast and at 8:45 he leaves the house.

   School begins at 9:00 and Paul is usually late. When he gets there at 9:15, his friends are busy at work.

   At 12:00 Paul is tired and hungry, and he and his friends go to the school cafeteria for lunch. They sit and talk and do their homework.

   At 12:30 Paul's mathematics class begins, and at 2:00 he studies science. Mathematics and science are Paul's favorite subjects, but he's glad when it's 3:00 and he can go home.

1. What time does Paul get up every day? _____ *He gets up at 8:00.* _____

2. What does he do at 8:30? _____

3. What time does he leave the house? _____

4. What time does school begin? _____

5. What time does he eat lunch? _____

6. What time does his mathematics class begin? _____

7. What does he do at 2:00? _____

8. What does he do at 3:00? _____

M. YOUR DAY

Answer in complete sentences.

1. What time do you usually get up? ....

2. What do you do after you get up? ....

3. What time do you usually leave for school/work? ....

4. What time do you usually have lunch? ....

5. What time do you get home from school/work? ....

6. What time do you usually have dinner? ....

7. What do you usually do after dinner? ....

    ....

8. What time do you usually go to bed? ....

A.

Ex. John _____*wants to go skiing*_____, but

_____*he can't.*_____ He _____*has to study.*_____

1. Bob and Jane _____, but

_____. They _____.

2. I _____, but

_____. I _____.

3. Mrs. Brown _____, but

_____. She _____.

B. Fill in the blanks.

| is | are | do | does |

Ex. When ___*is*___ Bob going to eat dinner?

1. When _____ you going to wash your clothes?

2. _____ I have to go to the doctor?

3. What _____ Mary have to do this week?

4. Where _____ you want to live?

5. What _____ Mr. and Mrs. Jones going to do tomorrow?

6. When _____ Robert going to go to London?

C.

Ex. Jane wants to drink champagne. _____*She doesn't want to drink*_____ lemonade.

Peter is going to fix the sink. _____*He isn't going to fix*_____ the car.

1. Bob wants to study English. _____ French.

2. We're going to get up at 8:00. _____ at 9:00.

3. Sally and Fred can play soccer. _____ tennis.

4. I'm going to wash the dishes. _____ the clothes.

5. Ted can speak Russian. _____ Swedish.

6. Judy has to cook dinner. _____ lunch.

D.

Every day Charlie eats breakfast at 7:00. At 7:30 he washes the dishes, and at 8:00 he goes to work. At 12:00 Charlie reads the newspaper, and at 12:30 he calls his wife.

What's Charlie going to do tomorrow?

Tomorrow Charlie _____*is going to eat*_____ breakfast at 7:00. At 7:30 he's

_____ the dishes, and at 8:00 _____ to

work. At 12:00 _____ the newspaper, and at 12:30

_____ his wife.

E. Write the question.

What	When	Where

Ex. I'm going to fix my car <u>next week</u>.   *When are you going to fix your car?*

1. He's going to <u>plant flowers</u> tomorrow. _____

2. They're going to work <u>in Boston</u> next summer. _____

3. She's going to study <u>Spanish</u> next year. _____

4. I'm going to <u>visit my uncle</u> next week. _____

F. What time is it?

Ex. It's three o'clock.   1. It's two thirty.   2. It's four fifteen.

3. It's six forty-five.   4. It's noon.   5. It's a quarter after seven.

G. LISTEN

Listen to the story. Fill in the correct times.

English	8:15	French	_____
mathematics	_____	science	_____
lunch	_____	music	_____

86

A. ALL MY FRIENDS ARE SICK

backache	earache	sore throat	toothache
cold	headache	stomachache	

All my friends are sick today.

                 Hilda      George

John   Margaret   Walter   Hilda   Linda   George

1. What's the matter with John?   _____ *He has a toothache.* _____

2. What's the matter with Linda?   _____

3. _____ Walter?   _____

4. _____ Margaret?   _____

5. _____ George?   _____

6. _____ Hilda?   _____

7. What's the matter with you?   _____

B. LISTEN

Listen to the story. Write the correct number next to each picture.

1

87

C. WHAT DID YOU DO YESTERDAY?

Write the sentence and then say it.

clean	listen	skate	wash
cook	paint	study	watch
fix	plant	visit	work
	play		

1. _____*I played*_____ the piano .

2. _____

3. _____ my living room.

4. _____ TV.

5. _____ English.

6. _____ my apartment.

7. _____ flowers.

8. _____ dinner.

9. _____

10. _____ my car.

11. _____ my friend in
the hospital.

12. _____ to the radio,
and _____ my
clothes.

D. LISTEN

Listen to each sentence. Put a circle around the correct word.

Ex. I play baseball.
| yesterday |
| (every day) |

I played baseball.
| (yesterday) |
| every day |

| 1. | yesterday |
| | every day |

| 2. | yesterday |
| | every day |

| 3. | yesterday |
| | every day |

| 4. | yesterday |
| | every day |

| 5. | yesterday |
| | every day |

| 6. | yesterday |
| | every day |

| 7. | yesterday |
| | every day |

| 8. | yesterday |
| | every day |

| 9. | yesterday |
| | every day |

| 10. | yesterday |
| | every day |

| 11. | yesterday |
| | every day |

| 12. | yesterday |
| | every day |

| 13. | yesterday |
| | every day |

| 14. | yesterday |
| | every day |

| 15. | yesterday |
| | every day |

E. JOHN'S DAY AT HOME

bake	cook	fix	paint	plant	rest	wash

John worked at home all day. His family is very happy.

1. Thank you, John. This is a very good dinner.

2. This is a wonderful apple pie, John.

3. The new flowers in the garden are beautiful.

4. Look at the car. It's really clean. Thank you.

5. The bedroom looks beautiful. Blue is my favorite color.

6. The TV isn't broken! I can watch my favorite TV program tonight.

What did John do?

1. _____*He cooked dinner.*_____   2. _____

3. _____   4. _____

5. _____   6. _____

What did John do after dinner?

7. _____

F. WHAT DID EVERYBODY DO?

bake	play baseball	wait for the bus
dance	skate	work
paint the bathroom	study	

1. What did David do today?

_____*He worked*_____ all day.

2. What did Billy and his father do yesterday?

_____

all afternoon.

3. What did Fred do yesterday?

_____

all afternoon.

4. What did Mr. and Mrs. Smith do yesterday?

_____

all evening.

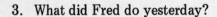

5. What did Shirley do today?

_____

all afternoon.

6. What did you and your husband do yesterday?

_____

all afternoon.

7. _____ Nancy _____ today?

_____ all afternoon.

8. _____ Mr. and Mrs. Wilson

_____ yesterday ?

_____ all day.

G. BILL'S WEDDING

Fill in the missing words.

At Bill's wedding last night, my father (play) ____played____ the piano, and my mother (sing) _____ popular songs. My little sister Sara (eat) _____ cookies and candy all night.

My brother Peter is a wonderful dancer. Last night he (dance) _____ with all my cousins and all my aunts.

My uncle John never dances, but last night he (drink) _____ champagne and vodka, and after that he (dance) _____ with every woman in the room.

Aunt Helen and Uncle David always sit and talk at parties. At Bill's wedding they (sit) _____ on the sofa together and (talk) _____ about their children all night. Bill's grandmother (sit) _____ next to them and (cry) _____.

What did I do at Bill's wedding? I (drink) _____ champagne and I (smoke) _____ cigarettes.

H. THE DAY AFTER BILL'S WEDDING

1. Peter has a backache this morning. Why?

    _____*Because he danced with all his cousins and all his aunts last night.*_____

2. Sara has a stomachache this morning. Why?

    _____

3. Uncle John is very embarrassed this morning. Why?

    _____

4. Aunt Helen has a sore throat this morning. Why?

    _____

5. I have a headache and a sore throat this morning. Why?

    _____

92

A. CORRECT THE SENTENCE

16

1. My sister fixed the TV this morning.

    _____
    She didn't fix the TV.

    _____
    She fixed the car.

2. Mr. and Mrs. Nelson painted their bedroom yesterday morning.

    _____

    _____

3. William washed the clothes this morning.

    _____

    _____

4. Our neighbors played chess yesterday evening.

    _____

    _____

Hello, Aunt Helen.

5. Bob talked to his uncle yesterday evening.

    _____

    _____

6. Peggy waited for the train this morning.

    _____

    _____

7. Maria studied mathematics this evening.

    _____

    _____

8. Mr. Jones called the doctor yesterday afternoon.

    _____

    _____

93

SALLY AND HER BROTHER

B. LISTEN

Listen to the story. Write the missing words.

Sally is very tired today. She (1) _____worked_____ all day yesterday, and her family didn't

(2) _____ her. Yesterday morning she (3) _____ the car. Yesterday afternoon she

(4) _____ the bathroom. Yesterday evening she (5) _____ the basement. She didn't

(6) _____ all day.

Sally's brother isn't very tired today. Yesterday he didn't (7) _____ . He didn't

(8) _____ the car. He didn't (9) _____ the bathroom, and he didn't

(10) _____ the basement. What did he do? He (11) _____ on the telephone all

morning. He (12) _____ to music all afternoon, and he (13) _____ in front

of the TV all evening.

C. WRITE ABOUT SALLY AND HER BROTHER

1. Did Sally work all day yesterday? _____Yes, she did._____

2. Did her brother work all day yesterday? _____

3. Did Sally fix the car yesterday morning? _____

4. Did her brother talk on the telephone yesterday morning? _____

5. Did Sally talk on the telephone yesterday morning?_____

6. _Did_____Sally_____fix___ the car yesterday morning? Yes, she did.

7. _____ the bathroom yesterday afternoon? Yes, she did.

8. _____ to music yesterday afternoon? Yes, he did.

9. _____ the basement after dinner? No, he didn't.

10. _____ in front of the TV yesterday evening? No, she didn't.

11. _____ the basement yesterday evening? Yes, she did.

94

D. YESTERDAY

1. Henry usually takes the bus.

    He ___*didn't*___ ___*take*___ the bus yesterday.

    He ___*took*___ the subway.

2. Julie usually buys candy.

    She _____ _____ candy yesterday.

    She _____ cookies.

3. Mr. and Mrs. Smith usually go jogging.

    They _____ _____ jogging yesterday.

    They _____ swimming.

4. Sara usually writes to her mother.

    She _____ _____ to her mother yesterday.

    She _____ to her father.

5. Peter and George usually get up at 7:00.

    They _____ _____ _____ at 7:00 yesterday.

    They _____ _____ at 9:00.

6. I usually have dinner at 6:00.

    I _____ _____ dinner at 6:00 yesterday.

    I _____ dinner at 8:00.

7. Paul usually reads novels.

    He _____ _____ a novel yesterday.

    He _____ poetry.

8. George and Peter usually do their homework at 4:00.

    They _____ _____ their homework at 4:00 yesterday.

    They _____ their homework after dinner.

9. Charlie usually eats at home.

    He _____ _____ at home yesterday.

    He _____ at a Chinese restaurant.

10. I usually drink tea.

    I _____ _____ tea yesterday.

    I _____ coffee.

11. Walter usually sits next to John.

    He _____ _____ next to John yesterday.

    He _____ next to Nancy.

12. David and Barbara usually sing popular songs.

    They _____ _____ popular songs yesterday.

    They _____ old songs.

13. Jane usually takes a shower.

    She _____ _____ a shower yesterday.

    She _____ a bath.

14. We usually go to a movie on Saturday.

    We _____ _____ to a movie yesterday.

    We _____ to a concert.

15. Mr. and Mrs. Wilson usually buy Mexican coffee.

    They _____ _____ Mexican coffee yesterday.

    They _____ French coffee.

16. Jim usually has lunch with his brother.

    He _____ _____ lunch with his brother yesterday.

    He _____ lunch with his boss.

95

E. WHAT'S THE QUESTION?

1. _____Did you go_____ to the bank?   No, I didn't. I went to the post office.

2. _____ a car?   No, he didn't. He bought a bicycle.

3. _____ to their uncle?   No, they didn't. They wrote to their sister.

4. _____ a stomachache?   No, she didn't. She had a cold.

5. _____ at 9:00?   No, I didn't. I got up at 11:00.

6. _____ today's newspaper?   No, I didn't. I read yesterday's newspaper.

7. _____ bowling?   No, we didn't. We went dancing.

8. _____ a good time?   No, they didn't. They had a terrible time.

9. _____ Italian food?   No, we didn't. We ate Greek food.

10. _____ a new shirt?   No, he didn't. He bought a new tie.

11. _____ coffee?   No, they didn't. They drank tea.

12. _____ French songs?   No, she didn't. She sang German songs.

13. _____ her Spanish homework?   No, she didn't. She did her English homework.

14. _____ next to Robert?   No, I didn't. I sat next to Fred.

F. LISTEN

Listen to each question. Put a circle around the correct answer.

1. a. She goes to the bank on Friday.
   b. She went to the bank yesterday.

2. a. He studies French.
   b. He studied Spanish.

3. a. He does his homework at 4:00.
   b. He did his homework after dinner.

4. a. I buy tomatoes.
   b. I bought bananas.

5. a. I listen to popular music.
   b. I listened to rock and roll.

6. a. He visits his uncle.
   b. He visited his aunt.

7. a. She writes to her grandmother every week.
   b. She wrote to her grandmother yesterday.

8. a. They play basketball at school.
   b. They played basketball in the park.

9. a. They go dancing on Saturday.
   b. They went dancing last night.

10. a. He cleans his room on Friday.
    b. He cleaned his room this morning.

G. BUT THEY DIDN'T

Bill went to a restaurant yesterday afternoon, but he didn't eat. He drank coffee, and he studied mathematics.

1. Where ___did___ Bill ___go___ yesterday afternoon?   ___He went___ to a restaurant.

2. What _____ he ___drink___?   _____ coffee.

3. What _____ he _____?   _____ mathematics.

Alice went to the supermarket yesterday, but she didn't buy any food. She forgot her pocketbook and had to call her mother.

4. Where _____ Alice _____ yesterday?   _____ to the supermarket.

5. What _____ she _____?   _____ her pocketbook.

6. Who _____ she _____?   _____ her mother.

Steven and Nancy went to their science class this morning, but they didn't study science. They ate candy and listened to records at a birthday party for their teacher.

7. When _____ Steven and Nancy _____ this morning.

_____ to their science class?

8. What _____ they _____?   _____ candy.

9. What _____ they _____ to?   _____ to records.

Mary went to a discotheque last Saturday, but she didn't dance. She met an old friend, and they talked all night.

10. When _____ Mary _____ to a discotheque?   _____ last Saturday.

11. Who _____ she _____?   _____ an old friend.

12. What _____ they do?   _____ all night.

97

A. A TERRIBLE MORNING

was	were

I _was_ very depressed last Monday. The weather _____ terrible. It _____ cold and foggy.

My husband _____ sick, and the neighbors _____ angry because my children _____ noisy.

The house _____ dirty. There _____ dishes in the sink. My children's clothes

_____ on the floor in their bedroom, and our refrigerator _____ broken. I _____ tired

and hungry all morning.

B. A BEAUTIFUL MORNING

was	were

I _____ very happy yesterday morning. The weather _____ beautiful. It _____ warm and

sunny. There _____ flowers in the garden. There _____ a bird at the window. My children

_____ at school, and my husband and I _____ on vacation.

C. LISTEN

Listen to each sentence. Put a circle around the word you hear.

1. (is) / was

5. is / was

9. is / was

2. is / was

6. are / were

10. is / was

3. are / were

7. are / were

11. are / were

4. is / was

8. are / were

12. are / were

98

D. BEFORE AND NOW

beautiful	expensive	heavy
cold	full	tired
dirty	happy	quiet

1. Before I painted my room, it _was_ ugly.

Now _it's_ _beautiful_.

2. Before I worked at Stanley's Restaurant, I _____ thin.

Now _____ _____.

3. Last week the weather _____ warm.

Now _____ _____.

4. Before Mary met her husband, she _____ always sad.

Now _____ _____.

5. When our children _____ young, they _____ always noisy.

Now _____ _____.

6. Before we had dinner, we _____ hungry.

Now _____ _____.

7. When I _____ young, coffee _____ cheap.

Now _____ _____.

8. Before Jack worked in a garage, his clothes _____ always clean.

Now _____ _____.

9. Before we got married, you _____ energetic.

Now _____ always _____.

E. A THIEF STOLE A CAR

was	were	wasn't	weren't

A thief stole an expensive car from a garage on Main Street last Sunday at 5:00. Mr. and Mrs. Jones ___*were*___ in a restaurant next to the garage. Charlie Green _____ across the street in a bar.

According to Mr. and Mrs. Jones, the thief _____ tall and thin. His hair _____ brown and curly. According to Charlie Green, the thief _____ young and handsome. His clothes _____ expensive.

The police are looking for the thief today. They're talking to Frank Harris. He's a tall, thin young man with brown, curly hair.

Police: _____ you on Main Street last Sunday at 5:00?

Frank: No, I _____. I _____ at home with my wife.

Police: Are you sure?

Frank: Of course I am.

Police: That's strange. Your wife says she _____ at home all evening, but you _____ there.

Frank: I wasn't?!

Police: No, you _____.

Frank: Oh, I forgot. Last Sunday at 5:00 I _____ with my friend Tom.

Police: Where _____ you and your friend?

Frank: We _____ here at the police station.

Police: Why _____ you at the police station?

Frank: We _____ here because at 4:00 last Sunday a thief stole my friend Tom's car!

1. According to Mr. and Mrs. Jones, was the thief tall and thin? _____ *Yes, he was.* _____

2. Was his hair blond and straight? _____

3. According to Charlie Green, was the thief old? _____

4. Were his clothes expensive? _____

5. Was Frank at home at 5:00 last Sunday? _____

6. Was he with his wife? _____

7. Who was he with? _____

8. Where were they? _____

9. Why? _____

100

F. ROBERT'S PARTY

did	didn't	was	wasn't	were	weren't

Robert had a big party last night. His friends are talking about the party today.

1. _Was_ Mary at the party last night?

Yes, she _____, but she _____ have a good time.

Why not?

Robert _____ dance with her.

She _____ very angry at him.

2. _____ you have a good time at the party last night?

No, I _____.

Why not?

I _____ like the music.

It _____ very loud.

3. _____ Fred and Tom at the party?

No, they _____.

Why not?

Fred _____ feel well, and

Tom _____ busy.

4. Why _____ you upset last night?

I missed the train, and I _____ late. When

I arrived at the party, there _____

any food. I _____ hungry all night.

5. Why _____ Betty leave the party at 7:00?

She _____ sad because her boyfriend _____ there.

6. What _____ Jane do at the party?

She sat and smoked. She _____

talk, and she _____ dance. I

think she _____ tired.

7. _____ you like Robert's party?

Yes, I _____. The food and the

music _____ wonderful, and

all my friends _____ there.

G. JULIE AND HER GRANDPARENTS

Listen to the story. Fill in the missing words.

A. How _old_ _were_ you when you _met_ Grandmother?

B. I _____ _____ years old, and she _____ eleven.

A. Where _____ you _____?

B. We _____ to school together, and I _____ _____ to your grandmother in science class.

A. _____ you _____ her with her science homework?

B. No, I _____. She _____ me. She _____ a very good student, and I _____ very lazy.

1. How old was Julie's grandfather when he met Julie's grandmother?

   _____

2. Where did they meet?

   _____

3. Where did Julie's grandfather sit in science class?

   _____

4. Did Julie's grandfather help his grandmother with her science homework?

   _____

5. Why not?

   _____

H. MISS GAYLORD

Listen to the story. Fill in the missing words.

A. Miss Gaylord. What _____ you _____ like when you _____ a child? _____ you very

   beautiful? _____ you _____ many boyfriends?

B. My _____ were pretty, but I _____ short and heavy. I _____ straight brown

   _____ and freckles. I _____ like boys, and they _____ _____

   me. When I _____ to _____, I _____ always embarrassed.

1. Was Miss Gaylord beautiful when she was young? _____

2. Were her sisters pretty? _____

3. What did Miss Gaylord look like? _____

   _____

4. Did she like boys? _____

5. When was she always embarrassed? _____

   _____

I.   GRANDCHILDREN

     Listen to the story. Fill in
     the missing words.

A.   How _____ _____ Tommy when he began to _____?

B.   He _____ _____ months old, and I _____ him his first pair _____ shoes.

     When he began to _____, his first words _____ "_____" and "_____."

A.   Really? _____ I tell you about my grandson Jimmy? He was _____ _____ old

     when he _____ _____ _____.

B.   Yes, you _____, but that's O.K. I love to hear about Jimmy. _____ old _____ he now?

A.   He's _____ _____ old.

1. How old was Tommy when he began to walk?

   _____

2. What were his first words? _____

3. How old was Jimmy when he began to walk? _____

4. How old is Jimmy now? _____

A. Fill in the blanks.

| was | were | wasn't | weren't |

1. A. _Was_ John at school yesterday?

    B. No, he _____. He _____ sick.

2. A. Why _____ Jane and Betty upset?

    B. They _____ upset because the weather _____ good.

3. A. Where _____ you and Lois last night? I called you, but you _____ at home.

    B. We _____ at the movies.

B. Complete the sentences.

Ex. Before we painted the living room, it _was_ ugly. Now _it's_ _beautiful_ .

1. Before I worked at Stanley's Restaurant, I _____ thin. Now _____ _____.

2. When Mr. and Mrs. Smith got married, they _____ poor. Now _____ _____.

3. When we _____ young, we _____ energetic. Now _____ always

    _____ .

C. Complete the sentences.

Ex. a. Barbara usually bakes cookies.

She ___didn't___ ___bake___ cookies yesterday.

She ___baked___ an apple pie.

   b. Robert usually writes to his father.

He ___didn't___ ___write___ to his father yesterday.

He ___wrote___ to his grandfather.

1. I usually have lunch at school.

I _____ _____ lunch at school yesterday.

I _____ lunch at home.

2. We usually listen to records.

We _____ _____ to records yesterday.

We _____ to the radio.

3. George and Paul usually visit their uncle.

They _____ _____ their uncle yesterday.

They _____ their aunt.

4. Jack usually goes jogging.

He _____ _____ jogging yesterday.

He _____ swimming.

D. Write the question.

Ex. _____*Did you get up*_____ at 9:00? No, I didn't. I got up at 10:00.

1. _____ to her uncle? No, she didn't. She wrote to her brother.

2. _____ baseball? No, I didn't. I played tennis.

3. _____ a good time? No, they didn't. They had a terrible time.

4. _____ the newspaper? No, she didn't. She read a book.

5. _____ to the movies? No, he didn't. He went to a concert.

E. Read the story and then write about yesterday.

Every morning I get up at 7:00. I brush my teeth, and I clean my room. I don't eat breakfast, but I drink coffee. At 8:00 I walk to the drugstore, and I buy a newspaper. I wait at the bus stop in front of the drugstore and take the bus to work.

Yesterday I _*got*_ _*up*_ at 7:00. I _____ my teeth, and I

_____ my room. I _____ _____ breakfast, but I _____ coffee. At 8:00

I _____ to the drugstore, and I _____ a newspaper. I _____

at the bus stop, and I _____ the bus to work.

F. LISTEN

Listen to each sentence. Put a circle around the word you hear.

Ex.
| is |
| (was) |

3.
| are |
| were |

1.
| is |
| was |

4.
| are |
| were |

2.
| is |
| was |

5.
| is |
| was |